SCRUM METHODOLOGY

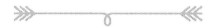

An Ultimate Beginners Guide to the Mastery of Scrum Project Management Methodology

SCRUM METHODOLOGY

Copyright 2019 by <u>Wesley Clark</u> **All rights reserved.**

This document is geared towards providing exact and reliable information in regards to the topic and issue covered. The publication is sold with the idea that the publisher is not required to render accounting, officially permitted, or otherwise, qualified services. If advice is necessary, legal or professional, a practiced individual in the profession should be ordered.

- From a Declaration of Principles which was accepted and approved equally by a Committee of the American Bar Association and a Committee of Publishers and Associations.

In no way is it legal to reproduce, duplicate, or transmit any part of this document in either electronic means or in printed format. Recording of this publication is strictly prohibited and any storage of this document is not allowed unless with written permission from the publisher. All rights reserved.

The information provided herein is stated to be truthful and consistent, in that any liability, in terms of inattention or otherwise, by any usage or abuse of any policies, processes, or directions contained within is the solitary and utter responsibility of the recipient reader. Under no circumstances will any legal responsibility or blame be held against the publisher for any reparation, damages, or monetary loss due to the information herein, either directly or indirectly.

Respective authors own all copyrights not held by the publisher.

The information herein is offered for informational purposes solely, and is universal as so. The presentation of the information is without contract or any type of guarantee assurance. The trademarks that are used are without any consent, and the publication of the trademark is without permission or backing by the trademark owner. All trademarks and brands within this book are for clarifying purposes only and are the owned by the owners themselves, not affiliated with this document.

Table of Contents

Introduction 1

Chapter One: The Basics 3

Chapter Two: Getting Started 22

Chapter Three: Scrum Events 41

Chapter Four: The Scrum Roles 58

Chapter Five: Scrum Metrics 80

Chapter Six: User Stories 86

Chapter Seven: Mastering Scrum 93

Chapter Eight: Scrum Management Errors to Avoid.....102

Chapter Nine: Methodology Comparisons and
Scrum Management Tools 105

Chapter Ten: Scaling of Scrum....................................114

Conclusion..118

Introduction

In this book, I'll provide you with proven steps and strategies on how to implement Scrum methodology. I'll explain exactly what Scrum is, its components and processes, and how to successfully use it for you and your business. Since Scrum is embedded in the Agile framework, we will begin by first explaining how it fits into Agile and the differences between them, which is a common misunderstanding. We will break down all the different elements of Scrum, including how you can maximize every part of the process through effective management and understanding.

You will gain an understanding of exactly how Scrum was developed, its underlying values, and the exponential growth in capacity it could provide to your development teams. You will understand the three main role players within Scrum: the product owner, the Scrum master and the development team. I'll teach you how each of these roles is integral to a development project's success. There are also smaller roles that operate within the framework that are all equally important.

A key element of Scrum, as you will read through the pages of this guide, is understanding the value of client feedback and using this to save time and money. This works hand in hand with the requirement of teamwork and effective communication within the development team. After working through this guide, you will have the knowledge on how to maximize the principles of feedback and teamwork throughout the development process to deliver the best possible product. While implementing this framework can be challenging, breaking the process down into stages and understanding each stage and best practice can be really helpful. At the end of this guide I have included tips for mastering Scrum, which tie all the elements of the framework together and will ensure you knock your next development project out of the park.

Let's get started!

Chapter One

The Basics

Understanding Frameworks

Before we delve into the detail, let's begin with the basics of development and defining exactly what a framework is. A framework is simply defined as a platform that provides functionality in a particular problem that can be addressed and solved. By providing this platform, before a development process is started, it allows the developers to process inputs and manage hardware devices without having to reinvent the wheel each time. The developer can implement the same method each for each problem the solve, regardless of what the problem may be. The Scrum framework defines roles and principles to be followed to assist and guide teams in a manner that is non-invasive and allows for regular adaptations and course corrections. This is one of the reasons Scrum is believed to be valuable. It provides options for different practices to be adopted so that, as a framework, it can provide structure to many different contexts. When applied well, regardless of the content or subject matter, the overall project and system will still recognizably be Scrum.

The Agile Framework

If you work in the project management or tech fields, the chances are that you have heard about Scrum or the Scrum project management methodology. This approach to project management is often confused with agile as the two of very closely related. Let's begin with a concise definition of agile and its origin before continuing to define the Scrum methodology and how it operates with agile.

Generally speaking, agile refers to the ability to operate in a way is allows quick and easy movement and changes. The agile framework originated from a brainstorming session between 17 developers, from different methodology backgrounds, who were looking for an alternative approach to project management. Their main objectives were to reduce paperwork and documentation and decrease the development time it currently took to produce outputs. This brainstorming session took place in 2001 when the lead time of software development occurred at a rate that could not serve a business's needs. They had often moved around the problem or found an alternative solution by the time a project had been completed. This meant that, even though some projects met their defined objectives, they still weren't successful in providing business solutions.

Prior to agile, waterfall techniques were popular in software project management and are still in use today. The waterfall model is more typically used in engineering design and breaks down project activities into linear phases that follow a sequence. Each phase depends on the deliverables of the previous phase being completed successfully, and as such, there is a high level of dependency between phases of a project. These techniques made little to no provision for feedback until the project was complete and ready to be delivered. For many projects using following these methodologies, there was little opportunity to course correct or receive feedback from the client, which would often result in a waste of time and money if the product owner or client were not on the same page with the development team. Operating in this vacuum is what these developers wanted to address and avoid by creating a whole new framework.

The result of this developer collaboration was a document called the 'agile manifesto.' Although the format of agile that we use today varies rather significantly from the original manifesto, the key output from this document was the recognition that the faster delivery of a product through regular feedback loops was the key to success in software development. The definition of agile, in its most recent form, is a software development methodology that accounts for the need for a flexible and pragmatic approach in the delivery of a finished and final product. Agile focuses on the complete delivery of individual components of software and not on the delivery of the full final product only.

The manifesto, which was created, outlines 12 underlying principles:

a) Use continuous delivery of software to ensure customer satisfaction

b) Be bold in making changes

c) Deliver increments of product which are in working order

d) Management and developers must collaborate and display teamwork

e) Avoid micromanaging and allow teams to self-organize

f) Face to face engagement is encouraged between teams

g) Measure team progress through the output of working software

h) Operate in short bursts to avoid team member burnout

i) Audits for quality and excellence should be continuously carried out

j) Keep things simple – stick to key elements of the projects

k) Teams are to decide on their own direction for the project

l) Inspect and adapt on a continuous basis

Keeping these key elements of agile in mind, let's delve into how Scrum fits into the agile framework and what the differences are.

What is Scrum?

Scrum refers to a framework that is implemented by teams or groups, most commonly in the tech space, who are collaborating on complex and intricate projects. This framework aims to ensure that the highest level of productivity and creativity is maintained throughout the project and that the end result is of the highest possible value. The starting point when tackling any project using Scrum is, to begin with, the elements of the problem, which are known or can be seen. This is known as empiricism. This approach is simple and useful when evaluating problems that have multiple or complex elements. There are three main pillars of Scrum project management, which are transparency, inspection, and adaptation.

Scrum was developed to be used by teams of 10 or fewer members. Although Scrum is most commonly used by software development teams, it can be used by any team needing a framework for collaboration. This and the fact that practices from other frameworks can operate in conjunction with Scrum are some of the reasons it is so popular and one of its biggest selling points. We will run through various scenarios and situations of when Scrum is most effective and where teams may face greater challenges based on the Scrum's underlying principles.

A Brief History of Scrum

The origin of Scrum is traced back to 1986 and a paper that was written by Hirotaka Takeuchi and Ikujiro Nonaka. Takeuchi and Nonaka made use of a metaphor, which stems from rugby. Scrum is a rugby term and is the practice of players coming together to change the direction of the ball. In software development, a Scrum benefits self-organizing teams in product development. At a later date, using the key concepts from this paper, Jeff Sutherland, Ken Schwaber, and Mike Beedle applied this concept to their own field of software development and further developed the theory around Scrum as a project management framework.

The rugby term 'Scrum,' by definition, refers to a play in which teams form a circle, pass the ball between them and aim to get it back into the game. After taking the original framework and applying it practically at the company for which they worked, Schwaber and Beedle documented their implementation and successes. In 2002 it was turned into a book, which was later followed by Schwaber's book in 2004.

In 2009, Schwaber co-founded the Scrum Alliance, an organization that provides resources and education on the implementation of Scrum. After leaving this organization shortly after, Schwaber founded

Scrum.org, an organization that manages the professional Scrum accreditation. In 2010, "The Scrum Guide" was created by Schwaber and Sutherland. This is a public document that defines Scrum and is the most referred to guide, which is revised on a continuous basis.

Scrum Glossary

Before we run through all the practical elements and components of Scrum, it will be useful for you to read through and understand the following glossary of terms used within this particular project management framework. You can refer back to these terms at any time to remind yourself of their definitions and how they operate within Scrum:

Burn-Down Chart: is a tool used to track the volume of work remaining within a project versus the time remaining to complete that work.

Burn-up Chart: is a tool used to track and graphically display how much work has been completed within a project.

Daily Scrum: are 15-minute sessions for the development team within a Scrum to come together to review and possibly re-plan the work to complete in the following day's sprint.

Development Team: form part of the overall Scrum team and are responsible for managing and completing all development work required to produce tangible outputs towards a sprint's objectives.

Emergence: is the discovery of new information or facts, which become pertinent for a project as it develops. These facts are often unexpected.

Empiricism: is a concept, which states that knowledge used to run a project is based on experience and known facts.

Increment: is a smaller element of a final product that works in conjunction with other increments to create a final product.

Product Backlog: refers to a list of maintenance tasks to be carried out in order for a product to remain in working order.

Product Owner: is a role within a Scrum that is responsible for ensuring the maximum value of a final product.

Scrum Board: is a physical board used to represent the progress of a Scrum. This is an optional progress tool.

Scrum Guide™: is the official guide written by Ken Schwaber and Jeff Sutherland.

Scrum Master: is a role within Scrum that is responsible for providing the team with guidance, coaching, and support.

Scrum Team: is a self-organizing team, which comprises of the Product Owner, Development Team, and Scrum Master.

Self-organization: is the underlying premise of Scrum and asserts that teams must organize their work autonomously.

Sprint: are defined events for one month or less in which work is completed and made ready for review. Sprints are run in repeatable cycles.

Sprint Backlog: is a summary of the development work outstanding before a sprint reaches its end goal.

Sprint Goal: refers to the specific objective or problem, which the sprint aims to achieve.

Stakeholder: refers to a person not involved in the Scrum but with a vested interest in its outcome.

Velocity: is the average amount of increment, which is transformed into a viable product by a Scrum team during a sprint.

Scrum vs. Agile

So, what is the relationship between agile and Scrum? Scrum is the implementation of an agile methodology, most specifically with its incremental delivery approach, which agile asserts. In essence, Scrum is an arm of the agile approach but also has a number of differentiating elements.

Agile operates at an optimum where projects include specialized development teams focusing on specific outcomes, while Scrum operates best for projects where requirements often change. This flexibility is one of the biggest advantages of Scrum, while agile, as an overarching framework, is relatively more rigid. The leadership role within agile plays a big role in addressing issues, and the progress of agile projects are delivered to the client on a frequent basis. Scrum differs from this by focusing on self-organization whereby all team members collaborate on identified issues, and the delivery of progress to a client is done at the end of every sprint. It is thought that this self-organization of Scrum allows for a healthier sharing of responsibility amongst team members.

With the numerous elements and frameworks that operate within agile, it is its incremental approach, which is the common thread between, agile and Scrum. Scrum is an agile process that essentially focuses on how to deliver the best business value to a client. Now that we understand the relationship between these project management methodologies, let's dive into the value of Scrum, its various components, and how to practically implement this framework.

Founding Values of Scrum

Following the initial development of the Scrum framework, five main values were added to the overall methodology for team members to follow and guide them during decision making. These values are often overlooked or not understood by many but are, in fact, instrumental in successfully employing the Scrum framework.

Courage

When working on complex problems, Scrum members are encouraged to exercise courage in making the right decisions on how to tackle obstacles. They are to support each other when taking informed risks so facilitate learning and the achievement of the highest standard of output possible. This value includes the notion that no one is perfect and that all available information that is discovered during sprints should be shared amongst team members to allow for optimum performance and calculated risks.

Focus

When dealing with complex and unpredictable problems, it can be easy for teams to lose focus. Maintaining this focus is crucial to getting the work required done and completed within the desired timeframe. Scrum requires that teams to work on a few selected tasks at a time and not elect for a multitasking approach (which is most often less productive, as we have already discussed). Teams can include this value in the sprint by aiming for a usable or "Done" increment to be produced after every sprint. Scrums rolls also have distinct accountability, which ensures that each team member is able to focus on their task at hand. The concept of addressing one task at a time is another example of how the focus is engrained in the Scrum framework.

Commitment

The collaborative nature of Scrum requires that team members are fully committed to the success of the project and be willing to commit to the completion of the tasks they are responsible for. Each member should support other members to ensure collective success. Through the way Scrum is set up, the various roles are also outlined in such a way that their commitment to the success of the project is unwavering. The product owner, for example, will show commitment to realizing and achieving the highest quality output possible. In the way manner, a Scrum master will illustrate commitment by virtue of their role description to uphold the Scrum framework.

Respect

Short turnaround times and the collaboration required to tackle tasks complex tasks involve teamwork, understanding, and respect between team members. This human value is crucial in a team's success. The Scrum framework promotes respect as a core element through the following characteristics:

>   a) All team members, regardless of role, are required to attend daily Scrums. This illustrates respect for the

work being carried out by each member as the value of what each person brings is considered equal.

b) The development team is required to wear many hats and often work across functions to ensure the success of a project. This promotes a level of respect for each team member's ideas and experience.

c) By requiring consensus on what "Done" means by all team members, the value of each person's input is clear. This is not unilaterally decided by one team member or group but by every person's input who works on the project.

Openness

The Scrum framework requires that teams work in an environment of transparency and openness where information is freely shared on progress as well as information, which becomes apparent as the project progresses. Not only is this openness encourage between teams and internal stakeholders, but also with outside parties and external stakeholders with a vested interest in the project. The requirement of consistent feedback loops plays into this value to ensure that all parties are on the same page.

Other elements of the Scrum framework, which promote openness, are the clear product backlog, which has sufficient detail to ensure all team members are on the same page. Once a sprint has begun, a sprint backlog is locked which gives peace of mind to team members that the goal post for the end of the sprint cannot be moved until the sprint has been completed. The sprint review and retrospective continue to encourage open channels of communication and facilitate an air of openness to honor this particular value.

Understanding the Value of Scrum

You wouldn't be alone if you thought that Scrum was limited for use in the software development space as this is where it originated. The great thing about this framework is that it can be used across different topics, departments, and projects; however, it works best for projects whose objective is to build a physical product. Before deciding what framework to use for your project and whether or not Scrum is the appropriate framework, consider these main value precepts:

- The cost of development is reduced: It has been proven that through the use of agile and Scrum, the cost of development is reduced. As specialist roles are removed in Scrum and developers take a versatile approach in problem-solving, there is a significant reduction of development costs. Team members are prescribed to have a wider skill set which allows them to address and solve a broader number of problems.

- Faster response times: With the current social climate we live in, humans want instant gratification and delivery. As Scrum operates in short and frequent feedback cycles, clients can receive updates and implement changes after a sprint almost immediately. Products will not only be produced at a higher rate but have proven to also be of a higher quality due to the incremental approach.

- A happier development team: With increased client feedback, rewards for your team will be more frequent. As team members get to understand the value of the work they deliver, shortly after delivering it, it fuels their motivation and speed of delivery. In addition, the fast turnaround times of products will provide your team with increased job satisfaction as products are conceptualized, produced, and out the door at a much faster rate than with other frameworks.

- Reduced Risks: Due to the incremental approach, whereby a project is constantly evaluated, and client feedback is received throughout the process, there is a decreased risk of project failure. With the short and frequent sprint cycles, the 'fail fast' approach of Scrum can greatly diminish the risk of spending time and resources on a concept that will ultimately fail or not meet the client's requirements.

- Better Performance Metrics: The metrics used to assess and evaluate a Scrum project are often considered to be more valuable than most other project management frameworks. This is due to the fact that cost and time figures are based on work already completed and the team's actual capabilities as opposed to estimates. Feedback on progress can also be provided by the development team immediately on the overall team's performance through the use of a burndown chart. This transparency of progress and reliability of metrics is considered a huge bonus of the Scrum framework. The metrics employed specifically through Scrum are covered later in this guide.

Now that we understand the benefits of using this methodology, we need also to run through the structural foundations are needed for it to function well in a given work environment:

Routine Tasks: Although Scrum can be used across many different fields and departments, it is not useful in processes that focus on the performance of routine tasks. Scrum operates at an optimum when complex problem solving is required for a specific project.

Common Objective: By the nature of the Scrum methodology framework and its close collaboration towards a common objective or goal, this clear objective is crucial. The product vision or strategy will usually outline the common goal in the field of software development. In marketing, as a contrasting example, the common objective may be derived from a brand strategy or specific marketing campaign. Whatever the objective may be, a vital requirement is that it is clear and understood by all team members and reiterated throughout the development process.

Challenging Tasks: In addition to working towards a common objective, the Scrum methodology requires that the problem at hand is challenging enough that it requires a team to work together to solve the problem. If team members can work in solos, without interacting with others and still contribute to the common goal, they will most likely refrain from collaborating, as it is not needed. The complexity of the problem or project must require teamwork and the use of teams. Without this, Scrum is an unnecessary framework to implement and could be a costly option when a simple project could be solved by a few team members which a less collaborative approach.

Remove the Multi-tasking Element: Traditionally, assigning team members multiple tasks and requiring them to multi-task was thought to be the most productive way to run a project. Team members would strive to have this skill. However, over time, multi-tasking has shown to be less productive as teams and individual members lose capacity.

As a team member switches from one task to another and 'changes gear', they lose momentum and focus. There may also be additional bottlenecks as tasks get picked up and dropped on a regular basis. Multi-tasking has also been proven to result in an increased number of mistakes as team members forget details through the change in focus. Thus, for the Scrum framework to operate efficiently, it requires that team members are dedicated to a single team and are therefore have dedicated team members.

Stable Team Membership: Scrum works at an optimum in environments where teams remain stable, and team members get used to working together. It can take up to 8 months for a team to really achieve a desirable cadence in working on projects collectively. When team members are dropped from a team, capacity is reduced, and it usually takes a few months for the team to get back in its stride. However, the loss of certain members may mean that the team never makes a full recovery, for whatever reason resulting in consistently lower performance. If you are planning to implement the Scrum framework, ensure that your team will be as stable as possible with little to no attrition.

Low Cost: Since 2001 and the development of agile, the cost of software development has been drastically reduced. Previously, the cost to make changes to software was extremely costly and, in many cases, as a result, impossible. Agile allows for low costs of change, even late in the development process. Processes that have allowed for this reduction in cost are test-driven development, continuous integration, behavior-driven development, and development operations. For projects that require changes that often come at a high cost, agile or Scrum are not as practical.

Plannable: Scrums usually vary between two to four-week sprints. During these sprints, work is planned out and allocated to each week. and to each day. and in some cases, to each hour. Usually, software development teams will make provision for additional time to fix any production or support issues. One limit of Scrum is that at least half of the work of the project needs to be definable and plannable to be allocated to each day of the sprint. For projects, which involve more uncertainty as to exactly what tasks need to be carried out, Scrum will not be a suitable framework to implement. If, for example, a company's business revolves around solving ad hoc client issues, Scrum will not be suitable, as sprints will not be able to be efficiently planned.

Autonomy: an important element of Scrum is that it allows team members to work autonomously, and with the feeling, they have the power to make decisions. This requirement of Scrum is explicitly required through the main element of self-organizing teams.

Skill Sharing: As with any kind of project or framework bottlenecks, for whatever reason, can have a drastic effect on a project's progress. Scrum promotes the concept that skills and knowledge should be shared between team members so that multiple problems can be attended to by multiple team members, leaving no single point of failure. An interesting practical example is Toyota, the car manufacturer. They dealt with bottlenecking by increasing pay for those employees who are able to work at a number of different work stations. That meant that employees who could solve more problems across more areas of production received a higher level of pay. Some other more regulated industries, such as healthcare, are also addressing bottlenecks by allowing, for example, a nurse to take on more responsibility or complete a greater number of procedures, which would usually only be done by doctors. There are, of course, industries where sharing skills and knowledge does not address bottlenecking as regulations or law prevent certain work to be carried out without an official qualification. The legal profession is a prime example of an industry where Scrum may not be suitable.

Early Delivery and Testing: Sprints require, by their very nature, that a useable product or increment of product is delivered at the end of every sprint. This allows for feedback to a client, as they can test and evaluate what has been produced and provide their feedback that will be used in the next sprint. If a team is working on a project that cannot be structured in this way, with a product being constantly delivered to a client (as opposed to one final product), Scrum will not be a suitable project management framework.

Limitations of Scrum

The Scrum framework was initially developed to operate in a highly collaborative environment and works well when teams are working in the same office space to conduct standups and effective sprints. The framework is not typically suitable or intended for projects where team members may be working in different countries or offices, as daily check-ins will not take place as conveniently than if the team was all based out of the same office. If geographically distributed teams are unavoidable, applying Scrum practices, such as the daily Scrum, will be more challenging and require adaptations and a more concerted effort. It's still possible to implement Scrum effectively in remote teams; it just involves more effort and coordination.

In addition to geographical location, Scrum is not suited for projects, which have specialized team members who only focus on one specific area of development. As Scrum shares responsibility and ownership amongst all team members, a versatile team is required so that different team members can tend to different tasks and elements of the project.

There are a number of other limitations to Scrum that, if combined with other project management methodologies, can be resolved or their limitation reduced. These include:

- Scope creep: this is the extending of a project beyond its original scope. This often occurs due to the lack of a definite end-date. However, it is recommended that when implementing Scrum, a Scrum master attempt to define or estimate a date at which development must be completed.

- Risk of project failure: Due to the collaborative nature that Scrum requires, lack of commitment from some team members could jeopardize the project's success.

- Scrum has limitations when it is applied in groups larger than ten members. Although this can be addressed by adapting the meeting framework, you may want to consider other methodologies if you require larger teams.

- If the majority of a team is inexperienced, it can be difficult to operate using Scrum without a strong and experienced Scrum Master. You may incur additional costs of educating team members and sending them on courses on Scrum theory.

- Daily Scrums can sometimes be frustrating to team members as they think it is a disruption in their workflow. It is important to set the expectation of front that the daily Scrums are crucial to progress and will take place every single day of a sprint.

Although this might seem like a long list of obstacles when it comes to Scrum implementation, thorough planning, and organization can assist in bypassing these disadvantages. A strong Scrum master, with good leadership and a hands-on approach, can navigate many of these challenges to ensure the success of the project.

Chapter Two

Getting Started

The Scrum Framework: Tools

If you have made the decision to implement and use Scrum for your next project management role, the great news is that implementing Scrum is relatively easy. It is the mastery of this framework which is a bit more challenging. In order to get started, you'll need to understand the various tools used in Scrum. Before we delve into Scrum artifacts, let's discuss the first starting block for any project: the project charter.

The Project Charter

During the planning phase of a project, the project charter is created. It is the responsibility of the project owner to negotiate and draft the project charter. It is compiled long before the multiple other elements of project management using Scrum come into play. So, what exactly is a project charter then? Traditionally, this term referred to the contract signed between the client and the company, which plans to carry out the development of a product. Over time, and through the development of Scrum, this charter now reads more like a memorandum of understanding that an organization may use between shareholders. It lays clear expectations of what is to be produced during the project and how the project should be governed.

The details contained in the project charter will include the duration of the project, the expected deliverables, the criteria for acceptance, the price to be paid by the client and any other details that are crucial for the team to be aware of. The charter is not a legally binding document and does not amount to a contract. The legally binding paperwork for a project will still need to be codified in another formal contract, usually handled by a product owner or project manager. The project charter, on the other hand, is a document that focuses on the good faith of the project, which enables all parties to have a clear understanding of what is being sought out to achieve.

When it comes to creating the legal paperwork for a project, this too falls with the product owner who may need to seek legal counsel in drawing up an agreement. This agreement will usually use the project charter as a reference document to ensure it encompasses all elements of the project.

Once drafted and completed, the project charter should be approved by both the client and any other relevant stakeholders who have commissioned the project. Once it has been reviewed and approved by the relevant parties, it comes into force and becomes the official document that will guide the development process of the product.

You may be wondering how you would begin to draft a project charter at the start of a project. There is no official template to follow, and as a result, the best starting point is to draft the parameters of the project as though you were drafting the memorandum of understanding for an organization. It should state and list all the clauses and conditions which the development process should adhere to and what the desired end product should be. The project charter should state that all stakeholders have agreed to the listed clauses and that each party involved commits to upholding them.

The project charter should also cover the course to be followed in the event that conflict resolution is needed. Although stakeholders may not anticipate that this would occur, it is important to make provision for this eventuality. Although every effort is made through Scrum to keep all stakeholders on the same page through an iterative approach and regular feedback loops, conflicts may still arise in terms of differing expectations.

Once the project charter has come into play, the entire Scrum team should meet to run through and discuss its contents. This is the starting point of creating a shared consensus and understanding between team members and what they are expected to do and how. In some instances, a product owner may, for the sake of clarity, create mini charters for each member of the development team, which outlines exactly what their responsibilities are. Questions may arise as to whether a particular task or activity exceeds or falls within a team member's scope of responsibility. Adding clarity through mini charters will address any uncertainty.

Scrum Artifacts: Product Backlog, Sprint Backlog & Increment

You will most likely think of archeology when you read or hear the word 'artifact.' As the traditional definition refers to an object or tool made by man or a 'work of art,' so Scrum also uses this term to refer to the main tools used within the framework. The three main artifacts for Scrum are the product backlog, the sprint backlog, and the product increment. These artifacts, or tools, all operate with the same objective in mind, which is to increase transparency and always ensure a shared understanding of the work. Scrum artifacts provide insights to a team, which facilitate understanding of a particular project and the tasks or activities to be completed. Let's begin with the three main artifacts as well as additional artifacts used in many Scrum projects.

Artifact 1: Product Backlog

The product backlog is a prioritized list of requirements, functions, and features, which a final product needs to include. This list is versatile in the sense that it is constantly updated by the product owner, and these changes are always communicated to the Scrum team. As a product makes progress and is delivered to a client in increments, the backlog continues to grow as feedback is received. The product backlog is the single source of agreed requirements for a final product, and the content and validity of this list is controlled by the product owner. Items listed on a product backlog usually comprise a description, estimate, and value and often described as 'user stories.'

As a key element of Scrum, the versatile and ever-changing nature of what is essentially a project's objectives, show just how adaptable and useful Scrum is as a methodology. This allows teams to operate within a framework that can accommodate greater 'environmental' changes such as changes in the broader economy, market conditions, or business and technology changes. As a project makes progress, a Scrum team will deliver product increment, which is tried and tested by the client. As feedback is received, it is documented and included in the product backlog. The product backlog can be updated at any point in time by the product owner or with the product owner's discretion. When it comes to time management, it is important to note that product refinement does not typically occupy more than 10% of a development team's time.

Backlog grooming, also known as product backlog refinement, is the practice of a Scrum team meeting after every sprint is completed and running through all the content of the backlog to ensure it is both relevant and useful. These meetings include every member of the Scrum team, including the Scrum Master and Product Owner. The objective of these reviews is to ensure the project is aligned with the product roadmap constantly. Backlog grooming may include some of the following actions:

- Review of the most important elements at the top of the prioritized backlog list

- Removal of elements which are discovered through the most recent sprint, to no longer be relevant

- Adding additional features, requirements or necessary functions which the final product needs to include

- Re-ordering items on the list as priorities of the overall project change

- Formulate answers for questions posed by the client based on the most recent increments delivered

- Ensure that all team members are up to date on the overall product roadmap and any necessary changes, which have been made or are still required to be made.

As sprints are concluded and backlog grooming takes place, the product backlog will become a continuing and exhaustive list. The items of high priority at the top of the list are typically outlined in greater detail than those that are lower down in the backlog list. Product Backlog items that be tackled in the upcoming Sprint are refined and discussed, and items that can be "Done" or completed by the team within one Sprint are deemed "Ready" for selection.

The Product Owner will make use of the product backlog during sprint planning to outline what items within the project are a priority. From this point, the team will define which priorities they can tackle in the next sprint. If you're wondering what a product backlog looks like, it is more than just a to-do list. Items on the backlog should always have the same characteristics.

- All entries should always add value to the overall product and to the client.

- All the entries must be prioritized in terms of importance to meet the overall objectives of the project.

- Items that appear first on the list will have greater detail than those towards the end of the list.

- Entries into the backlog are all estimations

- The backlog is a living document in the sense that it is constantly changing as the needs of the project or client change.

- The backlog does not include action items or routine tasks.

Let's delve into what each of the above characteristics involves:

Entries should add value

Every entry in the backlog must relate or refer to some kind of customer benefit or consideration in relation to the final product. Any entries without a clear client value should be removed. Instead, entries could include the exploration of client needs, various technical possibilities, any tasks needed to launch the product or any other functional or non-functional needs of the client or project. This could also include tasks relating to creating the environment, which the product needs to operate within.

Living document

The Scrum product backlog is continuously updated throughout a project. When necessary, new items are added to the list; additional detail may be added to existing items, items may be re-prioritized or even deleted. Although this differs from traditional methodologies of software development, this approach allows for maximum value for the client.

Detail differences

Depending on where an item features on the product backlog, so it's level of detail will differ. Items towards the bottom of the list have fewer detail than those at the top of the list, which is of a higher priority. The items, which are to be tackled in the next sprint, are the items that will appear with the most detail on the product backlog. The reason for this is due to the ever-changing nature of a Scrum project. It makes little sense to update requirements that are not part of the next sprint as their requirements will change before they become more relevant.

No action items or routine tasks

The backlog should not include items that are routine or considered action items. It only includes items related to creating product value to the client.

Items are Prioritized

All entries in the backlog are prioritized. This prioritization is done by the product owner and Scrum team collectively, although it is the product owner who owns this process. When it comes to this task, value-added, costs involved as well as risks are the most common factors taken into consideration. The Scrum master uses this backlog and the way it is ordered to determine what item should be dealt with next.

All entries are estimated

Items in the backlog are estimations by virtue of the fact that they are 'user stories' and by definition, need to be estimations. In many cases, Scrum teams do not have the information readily available to provide specifics for user stories, and so estimations are considered efficient. This ties into empiricism on which Scrum revolves around.

The collaboration needed to maintain the Scrum Product Backlog creates buy-in from all team members and ensures clarity of exactly what needs to be achieved.

Sprint Backlog

Definition:

While the product backlog refers to the product and end desired result of the project, the sprint backlog refers to the list of objectives for a specific sprint. The sprint backlog is the outline, completed by the team, of what specific increment or function is going to created or developed in the upcoming sprint. The backlog includes exactly what tasks need to be completed for a project to be considered successful.

As with the product backlog, the sprint backlog is continuously updated and contains a considerable amount of detail for the whole team to view and understand during the daily Scrums. As the project progresses and Scrums take place, the sprint backlog is updated and modified. As new work is added or existing items are amended, so the sprint backlog is updated. As work is completed, the estimate of work remaining on the project is also updated in the sprint backlog. As a general rule, only members who are working on a specific item on the sprint backlog can update its detail or amend its entry by adding or deleting it.

The sprint backlog is useful to team members on a daily basis as it provides a clear representation of the progress the team is making, and a real-time picture of what work is still remaining. Every sprint backlog should include at least one high priority item, a user story, which has been identified in a previous sprint's retrospective.

Updating the Sprint Backlog:

The sprint backlog should be updated on a daily basis without fail. All items for a project will be contained in the product backlog. A team will select a high priority item and break it down into tasks that can be completed in one day, and the task selected should be achievable in one day. As a team member, with a task you know, is achievable in one day, you will have an indication of your progress and whether you are ahead or behind rather quickly. This progress is then reported on in each daily Scrum.

Should the sprint backlog not be updated daily, it will become evident rather quickly that you are not able to see movement on the backlog and that work is being completed. You may also lose track of whether or not your team is falling behind. With the constant updates on progress, a Scrum team is able to react to slower progress and course correct rather quickly. Scrum teams who do not exercise discipline in updating the sprint backlog may not pay as much attention to the backlog and will be more likely to fail or veer off course.

What is in a Sprint Backlog?

In simple terms, a sprint backlog is a plan or guideline for the sprint. It will usually contain user stories from the product backlog, which the team aims to complete. Each item will be broken down into a prioritized task list for the team to execute. The Scrum team will usually use their current rate of production, or how much work they know they can complete within a given time, to predict what they can accomplish during a sprint. Once this has been estimated, the development team can compare the total hours for every task against the capacity of the team to do a final audit on expectations for the sprint.

When is the sprint backlog finalized?

Once the items on the sprint backlog have been selected from the product backlog and finalized, the sprint backlog is locked in, meaning no changes can be made. Once sprint planning is complete, a team can add but not remove items from the backlog. The product owner is the only Scrum member who can remove items from a sprint backlog if they decide that it no longer adds business value. During a project, items that are removed cannot be replaced by additional tasks.

What Is the Difference between Product Backlog and Sprint Backlog?

A product backlog is the list of user stories or tasks to be completed for a project as a whole. The sprint backlog is a subsection of the product backlog as it contains selected user stories, which are further broken down into tasks for the team to address in an individual sprint. During sprint planning, a product owner will select an item on the product backlog and clarify its specific detail. The team will then evaluate and determine if that item can be executed in the next sprint. What the team deems to be achievable is then added to the sprint backlog.

Who Manages the Sprint Backlog?

The sprint backlog is managed predominantly by the development team. It is considered the best practice to update this backlog on a daily basis so that the team constantly has a live reminder of progress, which is visual and keeps the team motivated. Should any obstacles or impediments to work occur, the development team should discuss this with the product owner as soon as this becomes apparent. Should any obstacles become apparent, the communication between the team will include managing expectations of internal and external stakeholders as well as possible solutions.

Product Increment

What is it?

Increment refers to gradual steps taken towards the completion of a goal. Product increment, in relation to the Scrum framework, refers to the sum of all the product backlog components completed during a sprint. These are combined with the increments of all other previous completed sprints. A sprint requirement is that the increment produced should be in working order and provide tangible value to the end product.

The specific definition of increment for a Scrum team needs to be created, and a consensus reached between team members of exactly what amounts to a completed increment of product. This will usually vary from project to project and team to team. As team members start a new project with the previously conceived idea of what an 'increment' should be defined as, it is important for the whole team to agree on what they believe this amounts to. Once the defining parameters have been agreed upon, this definition is used as the yardstick to determine whether or not the work completed during a sprint is classified as 'increment.' The practice of determining a collective definition or standard that the whole team ascribes to is a common theme in the Scrum methodology and is also used to guide the team when determining how many product backlog items it could reasonably complete during a sprint.

At the end of each sprint, as we know, the objective is to produce or release functionality in the form of an increment, which contributes to the overall product. Once the product owner has assessed the quality of the increment, they can decide to release the increment immediately or not. This decision will often be determined by whether the whole Scrum team believes it amounts to an increment of the required standard as required by the project. As Scrum teams work together over multiple sprints and mature as a team, coming to these conclusions is usually a much quicker process. In addition, the collective definition of increment may become more stringent, resulting in higher quality outputs by the team.

Who delivers a Product Increment?

It is the development team that will deliver product increments on a regular basis. This product increment should reflect the product owner's overall project road map as well as support the Scrum team's definition of "Done." Although it is the development team that delivers product increment and hold the majority of this responsibility, it is still a shared objective carried by the whole Scrum team.

Delivering Product Increments: Challenges

In some cases, Scrum may be implemented across companies with team members across departments. Breaking down silos that may exist, by virtue of differentiating departmental work practices, is often a big challenge and make take considered effort to address. It is important to get buy-in from the key stakeholders within each department so that these silos may be broken down. In addition to these silos, many companies will have their own work practices and values, which may overshadow a Scrum team, regardless of the Scrum's specific work parameters or values. Should any of these work practices be counter to Scrum methodology and how the framework needs to operate to be successful, the product owner will need to determine how to overcome these.

How is Product Increment created?

The product increment is created during a sprint as a result of all related development tasks, including design, analysis, testing, integration, and build. These actions result in creating a partial addition to what is envisioned as the final product. When using Scrum, teams will work on one feature of a final product at a time. It is planned in such a way that at the end of each sprint, a workable and value add feature is produced. This increment of product is then tested and integrated with previously delivered features. Prior to this testing and integration, a product is not usually considered to be "Done." Once testing is complete, the product increment is delivered to the client for feedback, which is taken on board before the next sprint commences.

This feedback allows the Scrum team to adapt and course correct. It provides useful input for a sprint retrospective and allows the team to decide, based on the client's needs, what the next sprint should involve. The feedback also allows for quality control checks and for iterative improvements, a key element of the Scrum and agile approach. The key principle is to use this continuous feedback to carry out effective iterations

What is the outcome of the Product Increment?

The product increment is useful to all team members for a Scrum, as well as external stakeholders. It allows a product owner to assess the current return on investment (ROI) from the final functionality that will be delivered to the client at the end of each sprint. Deliver increment at regular intervals also creates a sense of unity between team members as they receive regular feedback and recognition. The feeling of making progress and achieving success is a lot more 'real' than traditional project management methodologies where feedback is only received at the end of a project.

Definition of "Done"

When a product backlog point or increment is described as "Done," the entire Scrum team must reach a consensus on what "Done" means in the context of their specific project. This definition and what it means to the team, may need to be discussed at considerable length to ensure all team members, with varying degrees of experience and expertise, agree. This definition of "Done" for the Scrum team is then used to assess when work is actually complete on the product increment.

Just as consensus on the definition of increment will influence sprint planning, so the same consensus is needed amongst the team to determine what they collectively deem as "Done." Each sprint's purpose is to produce and deliver increments of functionality that adhere to the specific Scrum team's definition of "Done." As with product increment, as teams mature their definitions of "Done" are usually expand to include more stringent criteria for higher quality. The longer a team works together in a solid team, the higher the quality that can be achieved.

User Stories

The word "Done" is used most often by the delivery team of a project. In general terms, this means that a product owner has received an increment of the final product, or the final product as a whole, reviewed and accepted it. Once it has been accepted, this user story is marked as "Done" and is added to the team's progress. Examples of milestones or increments of product that could be declared "Done" are the acceptance of criteria which are met, the passing of functional tests or having code reviewed and approved.

Burndown Chart

At any one point during a sprint, a team can sum the total work remaining in the sprint backlog. In every daily Scrum, the team will track the total work remaining and the project the likelihood of reaching the specific sprint's goal. This allows a team to track the progress of the sprint effectively. A sprint burn-down chart enables a product owner to track the total amount of work already completed and that still outstanding in comparison with the time remaining in the sprint to do it. This is completed during every sprint review, and often more frequently. The information found during this sprint review through the use of a burndown chart is shared with all stakeholders of the project.

Let's run through an example to give you a clearer idea of how a burndown chart operates. As we know, a burndown chart is a graphical representation of the amount of estimated remaining work within a sprint. The chart will feature the amount of remaining work on the vertical axis with time remaining on the horizontal axis.

Below is an example of a two-week sprint a team has estimated will take 200 hours:

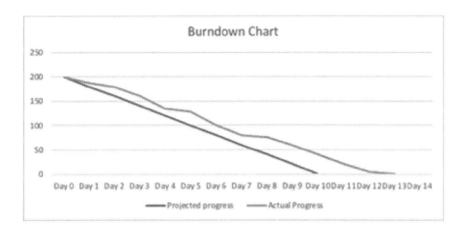

As you can see from the blue line on the chart, the team expects each day will amount to approximately 20 hours of work, i.e., after day one, they would expect to have 180 hours remaining of the project. In reality, tasks may take longer or a shorter amount of time, depending on progress. The additional days within the sprint allow for this variance as we can see by the orange line. This graphical representation facilitates and provides a clear understanding of teams of their overall progress, making it a useful tool for product owners. Let's take a brief look at both the advantages and limitations of burndown charts:

Advantages:

- Burndown charts are simple and easy to understand at a quick glance
- They motivate a team as they show the progress of the work already completed
- They give a clear idea of what a team still needs to achieve
- They provide warnings to potential delays or bottlenecks

Limitations:

- Burndown charts are limiting and only provide a partial overview of all the elements of a project.

- Tasks that are still in progress are not shown; only those completed. This means they do not always provide a completely accurate picture of how close a team is to completing a project.

- As a result of some of these inaccuracies, burndown charts can provide exaggerated expectations.

Sprint Goal

The objective of the sprint goal is to provide the focus for the team during a sprint. The sprint goal is the objective to be met within the sprint through the implementation and completion of the product backlog items. It provides guidance to the development team as to why they are building a specific product increment. It is the Scrum team collectively who determine the Scrum goal and what it entails. It is the product owner who has the largest interest in defining these goals, but the whole team is involved in discussing what these goals are. The product owner will provide input as is relevant to the overall needs of the sprint and ensuring the right direction is taken based on the needs and requirements of the client.

Acceptance Criteria

Acceptance criteria are the final component or artifact of a Scrum project and refer to the guidelines which a client has provided whereby a product must meet in order to meet their desired level of quality. If a project falls short of the acceptance criteria, the Scrum team must go back to the drawing board and figure out when it went wrong.

Acceptance criteria could come in the form of specific functionalities that the product should deliver, as an example. It could also be written as an extension of a user story or as a checklist. It is important to note that a development team should never provide functionality or features, which were not specifically asked for. Even in the event that the team feels that they could improve on a request from a client, they should refrain from doing this and only deliver what was asked for. The reason for this is that it may be more of a hindrance than a help if the client does not appreciate the features, or they end up getting in the way of further development that the client had in mind.

Acceptance criteria are listed in the project charter and are a useful guideline for the development team. Once the team has reviewed the user stories and acceptance criteria, they can get together and decide how best to achieve the desired results and how to break down the project. The autonomy given to a Scrum team to make this decision is supported by the principle of Scrum that promotes self-organizing teams. During this process, the Scrum master will only be involved as far as moderation is concerned. They will also take note of exactly what resources are needed to complete the job and ensure everything is provided accordingly.

Chapter Three

Scrum Events

We are now going to delve deeper into each event within a Scrum and how they take place in practice, including their various stages and requirements.

Sprint

Sprints are a process integral to the agile methodology and subsequently, the Scrum framework. It is a defined period of time during which a Scrum team aims to achieve specific goals. Sprints most commonly run for a period of two to four weeks. During sprints, a team will check in daily, keep open channels of communication between team members, and speak openly about any challenges they may face. As with any project, planning is crucial, and a planning meeting is the first step in setting up a sprint. During sprint planning, the product owner and the development team will review the product backlog to determine what specific items or user stories can be completed in the upcoming sprint. The development team who is solely responsible for the actual increment of the output produced, use this opportunity to provide their final input of how much work they believe can be accomplished during the sprint.

If the Scrum team has worked together on previous sprints, this recommendation is based on previous sprint velocity. The product owner is the team member who provides final input on what standards need to be met for the work to be in line with the client's or business' needs. It is the Scrum master who determines the duration of a sprint. Once consensus has been reached as to how long the sprint should be, all future sprints will follow the same timeline.

Sprint Planning

Before a sprint takes place, a significant amount of preparation and consideration is needed to ensure a successful start. Reviewing the product backlog is one of the first steps of planning. It is vital for the product owner to ensure that the information and detail contained in the backlog for the highest priority items are sufficient to allow the development team to execute on. It is the product owner's responsibility to ensure that these items or user stories are ordered in the correct manner so as to reflect the expectations of the client. The product owner should also encourage and facilitate discussions on the first review of the product backlog and get the team's input.

The development team will assess the highest priority items and provide an estimate of what they believe they can reasonably achieve during a Scrum. When a team has completed previous sprints together, providing this estimate is easier as it can be based on what was achieved in previous sprints. Sprints usually take place over a short period of time, lasting from about eight hours to one-month and are separated into two parts, namely objective definition and task estimation.

The objective definition is the first step that takes place during sprint planning. The product owner provides details on the priority user stories in the product backlog and explains them to ensure a thorough understanding by the team. The objectives for the upcoming being, being those items that can reasonably be achieved during a single sprint, are chosen by the Scrum team and the product owner. Task estimation, which is the decision around how a task is going to be completed, takes place during the second portion of sprint planning. The development team will then make a decision on the method most suitable to complete the selected item or user story.

As the sprint planning takes shape, all items on the product backlog will have been discussed in varying details depending on their importance. All Scrum members will plan and produce estimates for tasks, which they would be responsible for. If these estimates take up more time than is forecasted, it could mean that this item on the product backlog does not contain sufficient detail for the upcoming sprint. Work for the sprint is divided up between team members based on their skills and experience. Once the team has reached a consensus on what items will be included in the upcoming sprint, the product owner initiates the creation of the sprint backlog and burndown chart using estimates provided in the meeting.

During sprint planning the Scrum team, as a collective, will determine which items on the product backlog list should be part of the upcoming sprint. The product owner is must provide guidance through this process to ensure that the team is on the right track.

The end result of sprint planning should be a list created by the team, which details what they believe they can reasonably achieve during the upcoming sprint and during what time frame. This results in the determination of the final sprint objective. Once this is complete, the team can begin implementing the sprint plan.

Sprint Burndown

When the Scrum team has created and reviewed their sprint backlog, the sprint can begin. Individual team members will all carry out the specific tasks they listed during sprint planning. Although team members may work individually for parts of the sprint, there is still an element of teamwork and collaboration as the team band together to ensure all tasks are successfully completed. A team task board and the sprint burndown chart can be used to make a note of their progress and advancement as the sprint progresses.

Sprint Zero

The concept of sprint zero has created much confusion within the Scrum methodology explanation and implementation as it often gets confused with other tools and processes within agile. Many believe that sprint zero refers to the phase in which a Scrum team is put together or the phase when infrastructure related to a sprint is put together. Another misconception is that sprint zero refers to the planning phase within sprints. It may be possible you have already heard or read of sprint zero being defined this way. However, these misconceptions describe a process or stage within Scrum that occurs in the preparation and planning of a sprint, but do not form part of the sprint themselves.

So, let's move on to what sprint zero actually is.

Characteristics of Sprint Zero

The sprint zero team a group of high-level thinkers who are typically not team members of other sprints or Scrum teams. The main goal of a

Sprint Zero team is to create and deliver usable product or value that can be utilized by a sprint team.

The objectives of sprint zeros could be to create a project's outline, develop stories within sufficient detail to be declared complete and generally be lightweight in terms of workload or capacity. In order for a sprint zero to be successful, it requires that user stories already exist in a backlog for the sprint zero teams to use as a starting point.

Goals and Benefits of Sprint Zero

Goals

The ultimate objective of a zero sprint is the production of output, much like a regular Scrum sprint. One of the main differences is the level of detail and depth to which a sprint zero team engages with development. It is usually lighter weight and less intensive compared to a regular Scrum sprint. The deliverables of a sprint zero team could include examples, such as creating the minimal environment for code to be written by another team, or the prioritization of user stories within a product backlog, which will later be used by a regular sprint team.

Another way to simply outline a sprint zero is as a team that assesses and evaluates the readiness for a specific team to take on a sprint. The sprint zero teams could assess every aspect of the product required by a client to the environment in which the sprint team would collaborate. Should a company have a lot of experience in working in sprints and using the Scrum methodology, the value of a sprint zero team may not be realized. In this case, they could be omitted and left out of your Scrum methodology framework completely. However, should your teams be relatively inexperienced, the value of having team access to the development landscape before a Scrum team commences could be invaluable in saving time and catching unforeseen speed bumps from the start.

The specific activities which a sprint team carries out include updating backlogs, planning sprints, engaging in daily Scrums, partaking in sprint reviews and retrospectives and reviewing the final product to be delivered. You will notice that all of these activities are exactly the same as those carried out by a regular sprint team. The main difference to note is that sprint zero activities are usually carried out only over a few days with a week usually being the maximum length of an activity.

Benefits

Sprint zero teams give sprint teams an overview of the work that is to be completed. They provide a jump start for the sprint team who are to complete the project at hand. It may allow the sprint team more to insight into how to self-organize and perform more optimally going into the sprint. In some cases, teams may be thrown off or demotivated by unforeseen obstacles that arise a sprint makes progress. This can also lead to a lack of clarity. It is these issues that sprint zero teams can eliminate by setting the sprint team up for success by evaluating, planning, and reviewing the overall objective ahead of time.

Conducting a successful Sprint Zero would mean the end result would be setting up a team to start the first sprint of a project proactively. What this ultimately requires is the sprint zero teams have set up or ensured that an environment for development exists. Successful teams always ensure that their sprints take no longer than a week and the content or tasks they engage with are lightweight. These teams should also ensure they avoid scope creep and stick only to the tasks or actions which will allow the successful start of a first sprint. This sprint team can be influential in setting the tone for the first sprint, so it is vital that teamwork and a strong sense of collaboration is portrayed.

Not Just Pre-Planning

While planning and pre-planning are vital to the success of any project, carrying out a sprint zero is not a strict requirement. It is optional. Generally speaking, seasoned sprint teams have the necessary experience and thorough planning skills to result in s sprint zero being unnecessary. However, for organizations new to Scrum, this is a useful step in ensuing a successful transition to the agile and Scrum framework.

Sprint Velocity

Velocity refers to the prediction of the volume of work, which a Scrum development team can realistically achieve within the time dedicated to a specific sprint. Velocity is usually calculated by reviewing and evaluating the work a development team has completed in the past, and the rate at which it was completed. This makes sprint velocity a functional and useful tool when it comes to sprint planning. Sprint velocity of a development team usually remains constant during a sprint, which makes it easier for teams to provide an accurate estimation of when a project may be completed by.

The Scrum Team Roles in a Sprint

Later in this book, we will run through all the specifics of the roles played within a Scrum. As we are reviewing all elements of what a sprint entails, we will briefly discuss the roles and their responsibilities as they specifically relate to a sprint. All members of the Scrum team from the Scrum master and the development team to the product owner, have their specific day by day roles and responsibilities to fulfill.

Role of the Scrum Master during a Sprint

The Scrum master is the coordinator and works to ensure that maximum productivity from the development team is achieved. They are responsible for removing obstacles and protecting the development team from disruptions. The duties of the Scrum Master in a sprint include:

a) Coaching the product owner and the development team when and if necessary

b) Alleviate and prevent external disruptions from affecting the team's progress

c) Tackle problems the team may face and prevent them from affecting overall team progress.

d) Create an environment in which the Scrum team can make quick decisions.

e) Use every opportunity to enhance teamwork amongst members and increase productivity.

Role of the Development Team

To ensure the delivery of usable products, the development team are responsible for the following:

1. The selection and completion of high priority tasks from the sprint backlog.
2. Collaboration with other members of the development team.
3. Complete additional tasks as and when needed.
4. Report progress daily and complete peer reviews.
5. Notifying the Scrum master of obstacles or issues.
6. Successfully achieve the sprint goal

Roles of the Product Owner

The product owner is responsible for focusing on the content of the product backlog for upcoming sprints as well as helping the development team resolve any issues. Their duties within a sprint include:

- Ensure necessary funding and resources are adequate to maintain optimum development.
- Prioritizing product features.
- Represent product stakeholders in the Scrum team.
- Report on the budget and progress to product stakeholders.
- Provide clarification and decisions about requirements.
- Assess the performance of user stories and provide feedback to the development team.

- Introduce any new user stories into the product backlog as they become necessary.

Daily Scrum

Organizing the Daily Scrum

On each day of the sprint, the development team will come together to agree on the tasks they will need to complete to achieve the sprint goal. This meeting is called the daily Scrum and, as a rule of thumb, is not longer than 15 minutes long.

As the development team is the Scrum members responsible for the allocation to work to complete in a Scrum, they are required to participate in the daily Scrum meetings. This short check-in allows them the opportunity to review the sprint backlog, add any new tasks based on new information discovered, or share information learned during the sprint.

During these meetings, team members will describe the tasks they are working on and the progress they have made since the previous day's daily Scrum. Each team member will also outline what tasks they will be tackling on that particular day and bring to the table any obstacles or impediments they have encountered or anticipate encountering during the sprint. By the end of the daily Scrum, the development team will have a well-rounded overview of the team's progress, which they will use to plan for the next 24 hours of the sprint. It allows for gradual course correction and possible re-distributing team member's efforts dependent on their findings. Should many major obstacles present themselves, the development team has the responsibility of bringing these to the Scrum master's attention.

Should any major issues or obstacles become apparent that cannot fully be addressed in the daily Scrum, teams will set up a sidebar meeting in which to handle that specific obstacle so as not to impede the entire team's productivity and progress. As daily Scrums can run over time, disciplined teams will run these meetings with the use of a stopwatch or timer to ensure that feedback is concise and that the team stays focused. Another common tactic is for teams to use a particular object, such as a "talking stick" which m when held by a particular team member, gives them the sole opportunity to provide feedback. Each team member then gets their turn.

Sprint Review

As the objective of each sprint is to produce a useable and viable increment of product, sprint reviews are held shortly after a sprint to assess and evaluate the incrementing output. If a sprint has gone to plan, the team would have worked cohesively to produce high quality and viable increment of product. The team would have also been able to overcome identified obstacles and have resolved any potential risks, which were raised. A sprint will be reviewed and considered a success if the final output is in line with the product owner's expectations as well as the expectations and standards of external stakeholders.

The team will need to prepare for a sprint review by ensuring that they provide and present all the work they completed during the sprint. At this point, team members may add items to the sprint backlog so that an accurate representation is provided of the work completed during the sprint.

Sprint reviews are often confused with sprint retrospectives, but the two are separate events with different objectives.

Sprint Retrospective

A sprint retrospective is a scheduled meeting that provides the opportunity for all Scrum team members to evaluate the sprint process and create a plan for any improvements that are identified. A retrospective session takes place immediately after a sprint review and before the next sprint planning session. These meetings are relatively short in duration and usually do not exceed three hours to evaluate a sprint which took place over one month. It is the Scrum master's responsibility to ensure these retrospective meetings take place and that all team members understand the purpose of the meeting and contribute accordingly. Ideally, all Scrum team members should attend.

During a retrospective, the team may discuss the following elements of the completed sprint:

- The sprint's successes and want worked well
- The sprint's downfalls and which areas could be improved upon
- Improvements, which the team can commit to achieving in the next sprint

The main purpose of these meetings is to drive the goal of improved efficiencies and quality through the development process in the next sprint. It is the Scrum master's responsibility to ensure that this objective is at the forefront during retrospective meetings. The team will evaluate the work processes contained in the most recent sprint to find possible ways that the final product's quality could be improved. If required, the team may amend or re-evaluate their shared understanding of the term "Done."

The overall output of this meeting should be an agreed set of improvements that will be implemented in the next sprint. Although it is not a strict requirement that all improvements identified are improved immediately, a retrospective provides the formal platform for these improvements to be identified and made a record of.

While there are many different formats these meetings can take, one of the most effective ways is similar to the 'talking object' approach; allow each member the opportunity to provide input. This input is usually framed by asking each team member for what elements of the sprint they think the team should continue doing, cease doing or start doing. The Scrum master could also facilitate these meetings by encouraging the team to speak openly about ideas and brainstorm how they can improve as a team. Once a collective list has complied, the team will usually vote on specific items to be allocated to the next upcoming sprint. Following the completion of that next sprint, the next retrospective meeting will begin with a review of the list identified in the previous retrospective.

Whether you're new to the software development or Scrum or are more experienced in the participation of agile methodologies, you have most likely participated in a sprint retrospective. If done executed, these meetings will highlight opportunities for improvement and instigate positive change to elevate the team to a higher quality of output and performance. If these meetings are facilitated ineffectively or team members are feeling disgruntled, a sprint retrospective can provide little improvement should, for example, some team members be more vocal than others or elect to limit participation.

For the best results, a retrospective should be held straight after a sprint is completed so that the work is fresh in everyone's mind and new and relevant solutions are easier to extract. This should be a positive experience that allows for creativity, collaboration, and ultimately unifying the team members.

Sprint Retrospectives Benefits

If you feel like a sprint retrospective is just one too many steps in implementing the Scrum framework for a project, consider these benefits for your team ultimate success:

a) These meetings create a comfortable setting in which team members should feel confident to share their valuable feedback.

b) Retrospectives allow for teams to celebrate wins and recognize what they achieve during a sprint.

c) The list of improvements that come out of these meetings provide direction to a team, as well as an affirmation that the work completed within sprints is not only valuable in terms of the product produced, but also provides opportunities to learn best practice.

d) Should any frustrations exist between team members; these meetings allow these frustrations to be addressed so that they are not carried on to the next sprint. This ultimately aids team maturity and cohesion.

Sprint Review vs Sprint Retrospective

Both of these events within the agile methodology are Scrum ceremonies that take place at the end of a sprint. Although they share this similarity, their objectives are distinctly different. A sprint review is a meeting that allows the team to showcase the product and final output of the sprint, which was just completed. It is relatively informal, and the work produced is shown mostly to internal members of the team. That being said, these meetings can be elevated to include external stakeholders, in which case it would take a more formal format.

A sprint retrospective will follow directly after a sprint review and focuses more on team recognition, identifying what went well and what could be improved upon. This meeting results in a list of actionable items for improvement within the next sprint and also allows for brainstorming and new ideas to emerge.

In simple terms, a sprint review aims to showcase and demonstrate the output of the team during a sprint, while the retrospective identifies areas of improvements, which could be applied to future sprints.

Sprint Retrospective Challenges

Part of the managing team involves navigating the human element of teamwork, frustrations, and collaboration. Even with the best intentions and high aspirations, by the time a sprint retrospective is held, there may be a number of challenges presented that relate mostly to human behavior. Here are some possible scenarios and mays in which they can be circumvented:

<u>Lack of interest</u>: As sprints are held back to back and the team addresses similar questions in retrospective meetings, Scrum masters may find that their teams become less engaged in finding answers and offering up constructive suggestions to improve the process. This may call on the Scrum master to take varied approaches to keep communication free-flowing and avoiding feedback fatigue.

Emotions: Retrospectives should encourage members to provide constructive feedback. Due to frustrations, the unintended consequence may be hostility, negativity, and the blaming of team members. This should be addressed and diffused as quickly as possible. Although these emotions may be unavoidable, the Scrum master will need to be proactive in managing different viewpoints. It is important they remain unbiased to ensure the team always feel comfortable sharing their feedback.

A Lack of Conversation: By the end of a tiring sprint, fatigue may set in, and team members may be less likely to engage actively. This is the opportunity for the Scrum master to provide inspiration and kickstart retrospectives with interesting thoughts or approaches, which are relevant to the last, sprint. Another useful tactic could be to ask team members to make a note of their suggestions and thoughts throughout the course of a sprint and bring those thoughts to the retrospective meeting.

Five ways to elevate a Sprint Retrospective

Scrum masters can get caught up in the hamster wheel of sprint processes running back to back that they lose sight of what leads to team efficiencies. Sprint retrospectives can provide huge boosts to the way a team operates, and so it is important for the Scrum master to reflect on how these meetings are facilitated regularly. Here are five suggestions to elevate any retrospective meeting:

1. Keep It Simple: ask the team what they'd like to start, stop, and continue doing. Listen to their feedback and allow them to feel their feedback is being listened to.

2. Innovate: a Scrum master shouldn't be afraid to think outside of the box when it comes to running retrospectives. Teams will naturally get fatigued at answering the same questions in each retrospective. Asking questions in different ways or posing problems in different contexts can go far in terms of eliciting more useful responses from a team.

3. Focus: Nothing motivates humans quite like viewing physical boards that illustrate progress. In a world where everything is digital, don't under-estimate the use of physical boards with sticky notes. These boards can encourage collaboration and also accelerate a team's velocity as they become encouraged by the board being continuously updated. This psychology can create a snowball effect on progress.

4. Focus on Actions: The Scrum master should ensure that the output of the retrospective meetings is actionable items that are clearly defined and understood by all team members. If the items on the list are vague or unclear, they will do little to move the needle in terms of performance.

5. Make use of an agile coach: A fresh set of eyes and input on a project can do wonders for a sprint retrospective. Agile coaches have workable tools to ask team questions in such a way that it may encourage them to think differently about a problem. Although this is a rather costly solution, the payoffs in terms of output for future sprints may be worth it.

Chapter Four

The Scrum Roles

A Scrum has three main roles or responsibilities, namely a product owner, a Scrum master, and the development team members. These roles can often get confused with actual job titles, but these are not the same thing.

Scrum Roles vs. Job Titles

The three Scrum roles involve and outline the key responsibilities within the Scrum team. They are not job titles and do not replace existing job titles. A Scrum master role, for example, can be performed by someone with any appropriate job title. The essence of the Scrum methodology is to operate with an iterative approach that involves empiricism, continuous feedback loops and improvement. What is key for the above Scrum roles is that they are able to fulfill the objectives of Scrum by performing what their role requires. Taking on these roles does not affect their job title or other responsibilities within an organization

How to build a Scrum team

Scrum is an overall framework that different project managers can use to application processes. It provides the structure needed to run successful projects, which are complex in nature. While Scrum is incredibly useful in its adaptability to the different subject matter, it is not a one size fits all approach. As a project and its stakeholders vary, so the team members and the appropriate roles they should fill will differ. When building a Scrum team, this is something to be carefully considered. For example, a Scrum team working on an application for an online store will vary significantly from a Scrum team working on developing the integration of an Xbox Game. One will require technical knowledge of backend systems and ecommerce while the other will require graphics designers and sound engineers.

Depending on the complexity of a problem, building and selecting a team may be more challenging. Some projects may include many unknown variables that could leave a team without relevant and more specialist skills. In order to cater to a variety of challenges and subject matter, the Scrum framework outlines three main responsibilities to ensure most bases and responsibilities are covered.

1. The Product Owner
The product owner plays a vital role in framing a project and ensuring that it's key objectives are achieved by the team. They are responsible for the business side of the project in terms of accountability of the project as a whole, and to ensure that the vision for the project remains clear to all team members. One of the main tools a product owner uses to achieve this is through a product backlog. With a well-organized list of priorities which is consistently reviewed and amended as needs change, the product owner is able to control and steer the team's focus more effectively. Communication within the Scrum team is also the responsibility of the product owner. They need to ensure that all team members clearly understand the overall project's objectives, as well as any required changes that are made to the scope of the project.

The role of the product owner is best taken up by someone who fully understands what the final end product such looks like the functionality it is expected to offer. It is ideally best suited to someone who has a product testing or marketing background, although this is not a strict requirement. The ability to clearly communicate is the most important attribute for a person to have. They need to not only ensure they fully understand what is expected from the client but also need to clearly convey this message to the team and maintain communication throughout the development process. The ability of a product manager to forecast and measure what future market conditions may be or what competitors are developing may aid in their success in guiding a Scrum team.

The approach that a product owner takes in managing a team can also be a determining factor in the team's success. They should not take a micro-managing or dictatorship approach and allow the team to own their space and tasks with autonomy. This role should ensure they work with all team members to provide clarity when needed and continuous communication.

Another important responsibility of the product owner is to assess the completion of user story criteria within a sprint and whether or not it is "Done." They are the quality assurance measure within Scrum teams and need to constantly assess whether the quality provided is up to the standard, which is expected. Having skills related to making business decisions regarding functionality and profitability will also be pertinent to the success of a product owner.

One of the final key responsibilities of the product owner is to assess and maintain return on investment. They are required to view the project from the end user's point of view and ensure that the product being developed provides a credible solution to the problem they are trying to solve. The product owner will also need to prioritize the development of single features and steer the team with a clear vision to ensure the final desired product is achieved. They will be required to respond quickly and efficiently to any setbacks or obstacles, which the team may face, again highlighting the importance of this team member to maintain communication.

Even if all the other team members are efficiently fulfilling their roles, an ineffective or incompetent product owner can derail a successful project. They are, therefore, the cornerstone of the project's success. The product owner is involved in every step of the project and maintains this involvement throughout the project. They are required to wear many hats by representing the interest of all parties involved in the development process.

2. The Scrum Master

The Scrum master is responsible for making sure that every team member understands their specific role and the overall objectives of the project. Throughout a Scrum project, they will mentor, coach, and provide support to all team members while ensuring that they stick to the specific practices and theory of Scrum methodology. They should always lead by example and exercise patience while balancing the consideration of all aspects of the project and their task owners. The Scrum master works in collaboration with the product owner to manage the product backlog and find ways to ensure it is continuously streamlined.

The Scrum master is also responsible for ensuring that all team members have a clear understanding of exactly what is to be achieved and by when. This is a crucial task when it comes to changes within a project and the iterative approach of Scrum. They are expected to take any action necessary to assist the team in successfully completing a project. Along with the product owner, they should ensure that any impediments or obstacles to the team's success are removed.

A Scrum master should always be conscious of what a team can create within a specified time so that they can prevent a team from over committing what they can realistically achieve within a specific sprint. Over-committing on delivery can cause stress and anxiety within a team, something which the Scrum master should ensure to avoid wherever possible. This unnecessary stress will hinder a team's progress and lead to reduced productivity. The Scrum master should challenge the other team members to think out of the box in terms of innovation and what is possible. They should ask questions in a coaching way, which encourages team members to answer their own questions so as to facilitate the learning and development of teams.

Although the Scrum master is not responsible for the successful execution of a team, their role is vital in supporting and mentoring the team. They are pivotal in the backstage operation of a project. The most significant difference between a team leader and a Scrum master lies in the fact that a team leader physically leads the team while a Scrum master observes the team, ensures they adhere to Scrum processes, and that the Scrum methodology is successfully realized. The Scrum master should not interfere with the decisions made by the team around development specifics. Instead, they operate in an advisory capacity. They will only actively intervene when it is clear that the processes required by Scrum methodologies are not followed.

The Scrum master shares a responsibility with the product owner to remove obstacles from a team. These generally fall within three different categories with the first being problems which the team cannot solve. These problems could be delayed infrastructure, last-minute additions to functionality from external stakeholders or insufficient hardware needed to test developed products. The second type of problem, which could arise, relates to the unintended consequences of strategic decisions. Conflicts of interest may arise, or team members may be adversely affected by decisions that are made. This leads to the third type of problem, which a Scrum master will be responsible for managing, and that is handling the more personal element of leadership relating to the team members themselves.

3. The Scrum Development Team

The actual development of a product is carried out by the Scrum development team, who is a group of individuals who work together to develop and deliver a final product. This team could include team members such as business analysts, software developers, or product testers.

In order to ensure that these team members work cohesively, it is important that all members understand the common goal. This team is responsible for the actual product delivery and so also needs to answer for ant delivery failures but will also share in the recognition and celebration of project successes. The development team is required to report on their daily progress in the daily Scrums as well as share any successes or challenges they are facing.

It is usually expected that it will take a few weeks for a new Scrum team to get into its stride and deliver product increment, which is

100% on brief. Team members need time to adjust to working together and building interpersonal relationships that allow for great teamwork. This team has a significant amount of autonomy that they can decide independently how much work they can deliver in an upcoming sprint and commit to that accordingly. How a Scrum team operates in this may, by essentially deciding on projects and self-managing, is the perfect example of the essence of Scrum in action. The Scrum manager does not delegate the work needed to be accomplished. This is done by the development team themselves.

Scrum Master vs. Project Manager

Through all of these different roles and teams, you might be wondering what the main differences are between a Scrum master and a project manager. When overviewing the various roles of a Scrum, it may appear that the project management role would be redundant. However, the entire premise of Scrum is to handle the process of project management in an entirely different way. Traditionally, project managers were responsible for the ultimate decision making and the one who needed to take responsibility for failures. In this sense, a traditional project management role shares responsibility with a project manager. A project manager, by role definition, will make decisions on problem solutions whereas a Scrum master will provide coaching and guidance to a development team in problem-solving.

Project managers usually follow a more traditional approach to problem-solving. Essentially, Scrum works to distribute the tasks usually undertaken by a project manager, to various Scrum team members. This can leave project managers feeling out of place, but it does not necessarily make them redundant. Project managers still have a big role to play in the implementation and transition of a team in implementing the Scrum methodology. One key way in which a project manager would do that is through the training of employees in the transition and understanding of Scrum. They could either handle the training themselves or hire an external trainer.

Once Scrum has been implemented and is in full swing, it is the project manager's responsibility to assist in reporting and compliance issues relating to all projects. They need to ensure that the teams adhere to industry standards through compliance audits and the identification of risks. These are crucial tasks that are not fulfilled by members of a Scrum team, and so the project manger's role remains pertinent to the team's overall success.

The Project Managers Role within Scum

As you have read through this guide and the roles specific to a scum team, you may have started to question what role a traditional project manager takes on during Scrum. At first glance, it may appear as though this role becomes redundant when Scrum is implemented. The need for a project manager in Scrum is often debated, especially since the ultimate goal of Scrum adoption is for teams to be self-organizing and be able to navigate much of their development without too much guidance.

The role of the product owner and Scrum master, by definition, include responsibilities, which are typically carried out by a project manager, which is why the function of a project manager within Scrum continues to be debated. We know that a product owner is responsible for understanding a client's needs, benchmarking competition, and ensuring the development team has a clear picture of the client's expectations. The Scrum master is an internal servant leader and works closely with the product owner and development to support the development process while the development team gives input on what can be achieved within given time frames, and once approved, they work to achieve the agreed outputs. This appears to leave very little room for a project manager as the duties traditionally carried out by the project manager are done by the Scrum team.

Many of the roles and responsibilities of a project manager are covered by the three main roles within a Scrum team:

- Determining and setting the project focus (Scrum Master)
- Allocating Tasks (Development Team)
- Addressing any obstacles or issues (Scrum Master/Product Owner)
- Prioritizing the requirements of a project (Product Owner)
- Managing the project's risk (all Scrum team members)

Redefining the Project Manager's Role in Scrum

While it is true that Scrum teams can operate without the role of a project manager, a skilled project manager is still an asset to the Scrum management process. Project managers, through a diverse and valuable skill set, can fulfill a role within the Scrum team, whether that be as a product owner, Scrum master, or the development team.

Project Manager – Scrum Master

Project managers are skilled in communicating and negotiating with stakeholders, implementing change management, and managing timelines and expected deadlines. The Scrum master role is a popular one for a project manager to take on as the roles are relatively similar. If there are existing reporting lines between the project manager and the rest of the Scrum team, the Scrum master would not be a great fit for a project manager. This is due to the communication and feedback (and possibly pushback) that may be necessary amongst team members and the fact they may feel comfortable pushing back against their manager.

Project Manager – Scrum of Scrums Master

Large organizations may have many teams working on large development projects across multiple teams where coordination related to planning and testing must take place. Dependencies between the teams and possible roadblocks should be carefully managed. A Scrum of Scrums master has the responsibility of reviewing dependencies that may exist between teams and coordinate activities to prevent these from delaying the progress of the Scrum teams. This is a role that requires negotiation skills and advanced communication and could be great for an advanced project manager.

Project Manager – Programs Manager

Although the Scrum roles explained in previous chapters cover a large number of areas and duties required for development, there are a number of decisions or tasks, which are often overlooked. These include budgeting, hiring and firing, and performance reviews. Should disputes arise between the team, a person outside of the three main roles may be instrumental in reaching resolutions. This is a role that a project manager could undertake in support of the Scrum team.

As Scrum teams are built to be self-organizing and relatively self-sufficient, the transition to Scrum may leave a project manager feeling out of place. However, project managers often have valuable skills that complement a Scrum team and make the process more seamless. There are a number of elements of a project, which should be considered in determining how a project manager could fit into either of the three main roles or an additional support role. These elements include the scale and complexity of the project, the size of the project, the risk profile, the geographical location of the team, governance, and commercial consideration.

1. Scale and Complexity

Should a project involve a small team operating from the same location on a relatively simple project, a project manager is not usually deemed necessary. As we have mentioned, all of the elements of the project will be covered by the Scrum roles. However, projects, which are more complex and have multiple components place different demands on the team, and a project manager could be vital to addressing and undertaking support tasks that are crucial to the team's success.

2. Project Size

As a project gets bigger in size and scope, it inherently becomes more complex. Some projects may involve multiple teams and require an additional layer of coordination and support. For these larger projects, the support of a project manager is very useful.

3. Risk Profile

One of the benefits of implementing the Scrum framework is the manner in which risk is decreased through the iterative approach and opportunities for course correction. That being said, there are still additional risks that may present themselves throughout a project which require identifying, reporting, and being actively managed. The risks identified at the beginning of a project need to be monitored throughout, as well as focusing on any the identification of risks that appear as the project progresses. This bigger picture thinking when it comes to risk is ideal for a project manager to take on.

4. Physical Distribution of the Team
It has become more common for Scrum teams to be distributed geographically. In this instance, communication is more challenging and requires a more coordinated approach. While it is usually recommended that Scrum is not suitable for teams who are widespread, they may have few options. In this case, poor communication or not sticking to a daily Scrum schedule can severely affect a team's progress. A Scrum master might not have the time or energy, to consistently ensure those team members calling in for daily Scrums and all other meetings, which are crucial to progress. This is where a project manager could step in.

5. Complexity of Delivery
Larger projects typically involve greater levels of complexity, as opposed to delivering only a single software product. The Scrum process for larger and more complex projects may require large scale infrastructure and attention to changes in the business process. A bigger project and higher level of complexity require a greater degree of planning and structure, which can be undertaken by a project manager.

6. Governance

Development projects usually form part of a much bigger framework or portfolio, which is governed by a particular type of environment. This type of environment may not subscribe to Agile, making it more challenging to implement Scrum as the cadence of projects does not align. This may particularly be evident when it comes to reporting as Scrum reporting is usually based around sprint cycles.

Some Scrum projects may need to operate within a greater organizational environment where company politics need to be managed. A project manager may be the perfect buffer between the greater organization and the Scrum team. They could manage the feedback loops between both parties and ensure there is a consensus on key decisions. Although Scrum ensures regular feedback by nature of its principles, having a project manager ensure the feedback is digestible for external stakeholders could go a long way to ensuring the success of a project.

7. Commercial Considerations

With many Scrum projects, there are commercial considerations as well as contractual obligations that need to be kept in mind throughout the development process. In order for the development team to stay focused on delivering a high-quality project, it may be useful to have a project manager handle the commercial aspect so that the team can solely focus on development. While the development does still need to be aware of the commercial considerations, it should not be their key concern.

Now that we understand all the different roles within Scrum, here are ten practical steps for you to take in assembling your first Scrum team.

How to Assemble a Scrum Team

By taking the time and effort to assemble your first Scrum team the correct way, you have already won half the battle in ensuring your team is set up for success. This process often takes more time and energy than most people realize. It is unrealistic to expect that success can be achieved by simply choosing a team and scheduling some lightweight training on Scrum. It is important that team members chosen are carefully considered and that time is taken to nurture the relationships between team members. This greatly aids the team's ability to successfully self-organize, using each other's strengths to overcome obstacles. As a key player is assembling a Scrum team, it is important that you fully understand the process of team forming, and exactly what role you should be playing. In 1965, a psychologist by the name of Bruce Tuckman developed a model that explains how teams develop and gel in order to operate effectively. He based his model on the 26 studies he carried out on small groups, and through these studies, he identified five main stages of successful team development:

- **Forming phase**: is this first phase that a group goes through and is mostly concerned with the reason for the group's existence. What has the Scrum team been chosen to achieve and how could they achieve it are questions each team member will have. As this is the first phase of the group, many team members will not know each other and will yet know each other very well. The security, which usually comes with a well-established team such as being comfortable to provide criticism and voice concerns or irritations, does not exist during this stage. Similarly, a strong sense of belonging and unity has not yet formed amongst the team. In order to successfully begin the group development, the

Scrum master should take on the role of an educator to ensure each team member knows and understand their purpose and role to play with the team.

- **Storming phase**: As a sense of familiarity gradually starts to develop between team members, they become more comfortable in collaborating and working side by side. The openness and willingness to speak out about doubts, worries, and frustration increases as the team spend more time together. The first question which a team will usually address during this phase is 'who will do what?' and 'how will it be accomplished?' Small issues or conflicts may arise during this stage. This is a natural result of the differences between what team members expect from the process as a whole, both from each other and the team. If sufficient opportunity is provided to resolve conflicts and discuss any concerns constructively, the team will develop a sense of trust.

- **Norming phase**: The third phase of a group's development focuses on expectations. This expectation refers to that of the individual team members, as well as the expectations of the group as a whole. When setting expectations, the following elements should be taken into consideration: quality of work to be produced, speed and sprint velocity, and how each team member should conduct themselves within the development process. This phase contains more specific discussions on what tasks need to be completed, and a greater sense of community starts to develop.

- **Performing phase**: Following the previous phase, the team can build on the sense of belonging to begin working in a constructive group. In this penultimate phase, the team members start to become more comfortable with this role and feel happy to take a more flexible approach to their roles and responsibilities. The usual concerns and anticipation of being part of a new group should have mostly dissipated. The team members should be feeling more established and relaxed and ready to begin collaborating. It is during this phase that the Scrum master begins his advisory role in guiding the team as they hit speed bumps.

- **Adjourning phase**: This is the final stage or a team's development and involves completing a project and finding the solution to a particular problem. There is a relatively large human aspect in this stage as team members may feel somewhat at a loss when the team ceases to work together. This may be the case whether the team has worked together on many projects over a long period of time, or if they have only worked together for a short period. In this final stage, the Scrum master should be cognizant of these feelings and play the role of a facilitator when team members are given the opportunity to express their feelings and emotions.

The theory on group formation and the human element it involves can be extremely helpful for a Scrum master to understand and know how he can assist the team through each stage. Although this theory on teams isn't knowledge that needs to be passed on to Scrum members, it is helpful knowledge for the product owners and Scrum masters to have in the back of their minds as they develop a successful Scrum team. It is during these phases that the Scrum master should pay close attention to the team, their feelings, and how they are progressing both individually and as a team.

Here are our top 10 tips for setting up a successful Scrum team:

1. Kickstart it!

A kickstart refers to the pow-wow sessions, which take place before a Scrum team is officially formed and is a great opportunity to lay the foundations for a solid team structure. As it is intended to be a motivational and exciting activity, kick start sessions should take place at the beginning of the week or a day and not left for the last thing to do on a Friday afternoon. Kickstart sessions usually last for 2 to 3 days with the first day set aside for training on Scrum theory for all team members. The second day focuses on team building and breaking the ice between team members. The final day is allocated to focusing on the upcoming first sprint. This session can be combined with sprint planning as it is where the product backlog is created, and the first sprint is started.

Three days of additional planning may be something you don't think your team can afford in terms of time and resources. However, this sets the tone for the whole team and send out the message that, as a Scrum master, you take their development and success seriously.

2. Create Familiarization

Allowing teams enough time to get to know each other and placing value on the process is the sign of a great Scrum master. Whether teams have some level of familiarity or have known each other for a while, it is important for them to establish a different kind of interaction in the context of the Scrum team. As team members come out of their comfort zones, they will slowly form a sense of cohesion and unity as a new group. This stage cannot be rushed, and it is important to allocate time for it take place organically.

3. Teach Scrum

In order to ensure the success of a Scrum team, it is important for all the team members to have a thorough understanding of Scrum theory and all of the relevant components. Having one or two team members who have read a book on Scrum or have a vague idea of how Scrum works are unlikely to lead to successful implementations. With the increased popularity of Scrum, many misconceptions or interpretations exist on exactly how Scrum should be run and what falls under its purview.

One of the best ways to ensure that your team has the required knowledge of how the framework should be implemented, is to enlist a team in Scrum training to ensure all team members have the same interpretation of the framework.

4. Formulate a Team Vision

The 'norming phase' can be quite challenging, but a team can be helped through this phase by encouraging the team to think about and discuss what good teamwork and dynamics look like. A useful approach is to get the team to give their opinion on what a good team would look like and what a bad team would look like. Vocalizing the characteristics and attributes the team members value works to set the tone for the team proactively.

5. Create a Team Contract

When implementing Scrum, creating clarity from the beginning is crucial to the team being set up for success. A team may have questions revolving around how they are going to work as a team, who will be responsible for what tasks, and when will all the different Scrum events be held. Creating clarity on these questions, especially those related to roles and tasks, is important for teams that are in the forming & storming stages. As team members may not yet feel comfortable in raising some of their questions or concerns in these early stages, it is important to create as much clarity as possible. One way of doing this is to create a contract between the team members, which clearly outlines and answers the typical questions they may have. These questions may include:

1. How many team members will there be? Who will be a part of the team and what value to they add?

2. Who will take on what role within the Scrum and why? Who will be the product owner or the Scrum master and who will form part of the development team?

3. When are where will the Scrum events take place? How long will each event be and who is expected to attend each event?

4. What happens when certain members don't attend meetings they are expected to join? Or what happens when someone is late? This last question can be significant in Scrum as the timing of events is crucial to keeping the project on track.

5. How will the team decide that they are happy with the outcome of a Scrum? What criteria will be used to determine this?

The team should be allowed time to brainstorm the questions they would like answers to and then, subsequently, to answer them as a group.

6. Come up with a Team Name

As a team begins to form and work through the first two stages of existence, they will start to develop an identity as a unit as a result of their collaboration. The identity that is developed revolves around the method of collaboration, the values the team ascribes to and the principles, which they uphold as a team. Creating a team name could be one way of further cementing this sense of unity and belonging for the team and should align with the mission and purpose of the team. You are thinking that this might feel like forced cohesion in instances where the teams are taking longer than usual to get into their stride. In that case, it's ok to forego a team name until a later time when relationships are more developed, and the team is more established.

Picking a name for the team isn't just a fun idea done for the sake of it. It is a concept that is entrenched in psychology and which psychologists call 'mere group membership.' This is a concept that refers to how people, when being part of a defined and labeled group, feel a greater sense of membership and belonging.

7. Set expectations

It takes the completion of a number of sprints and possibly even a number of projects before a team develops good traction and cohesion while working as a team. Unfortunately, learning how to work best together is something that does not just happen over 1 or 2 sprints, and this is not a process that can be sped up. It is important that all the team members understand and anticipate that it might take a while for the team to develop decent cadence and cohesion as a team. One way to manage expectation is to explain the 5 phases which team development has and that it is normal for there to be teething problems during the process.

8. Hold a Retrospective and Repeat!

A sprint retrospective is a perfect opportunity for a team to address any of their fears or concerns and make a note of the areas of the project or team collaboration that is not working as well as they could be. However, a retrospective is so much more than this. This is a Scrum event in which teams often grow and improve the most and should not be skipped. Encourage team members to prepare for these sessions so that the meeting can begin with feedback, which is free-flowing. Some teams record their feedback in their individual notes throughout the sprint so that they do not forget their feedback by the time the retrospective takes place.

One useful approach for retrospectives is to encourage the team to all come with two positive comments on the last sprint as well as two negatives or areas of improvement. Usually, common themes will emerge and can be identified to be addressed in the next sprint so that they can be improved upon if negatives or leveraged off if positive.

9. Involve management!

When dealing with complex and challenging development, a Scrum team may go through phases of feeling demotivated or isolated. This is where the support of the organization's wider management could really have an impact. This could be done at the start of the end of the process or both. It is crucial that in showing their support that management actively listen to and communicate with the team. They should offer their support and ask where they could help.

10. Empower the team

It may be very tempting for a Scrum master or coach to solve a team's problems instead of letting the team address them themselves. It is crucial to the successful implementation of Scrum that self-organization is allowed to happen and that the Scrum master provides guidance without interfering or taking over the process. Every problem, which a team may face, presents an opportunity for them to grow as a team and advance their problem-solving skills. The role of the Scrum master is to ask the right kind of coaching questions to enable the team to view their obstacles in different ways so as to reach the most effective and workable conclusion.

Building a Scrum team is no small feat and requires a lot of continuous and concerted effort. Hopefully, the tips above will guide you as you build a team from scratch and develop the way in which they work together.

Chapter Five

Scrum Metrics

A core tenet of successful project management is using valuable metrics to measure the progress of a project. Without a quantitative measure of the project, it would be easier for a team to take a more casual approach without ever really understanding what progress they had made. Qualitative metrics, on the other hand, are limited in their use to measure a team's progress. Failing to use the correct metrics to measure success also makes it impossible for teams to compare how they performed from sprint to sprint and project to project.

Before a team is built or project begins, it is vital that the project leaders develop a series of metrics and indicators that will be used throughout the entire development process. Just like many other project management methodologies, Scrum seeks to use Key Performance Indicators (KPIs) to measure the success of a project and the quality of the output. It is the entire team's responsibility to track KPIs as a collaborative effort, much like all other elements of Scrum. It is the Scrum master who is responsible for collating the relevant information that is used to generate the relevant KPIs.

The development team is responsible for tracking their own progress. They should always be on top of how many hours they have worked, how many hours are remaining, and what work still needs to be completed. The product owner, although very involved in compiling KPIs, does not have the right to manage the process actively. This means that it is the whole team's responsibility to track and manage the project, not just the product owner or Scrum master.

As you can tell, there is no one role player or position responsible for tracking KPIs and performance. This remains the duty of all team members. Scrum metrics fall part into a broader group of KPIs for the Agile framework. Different metrics may be used for different projects, depending on the specific requirements for the final output. Scrum practitioners will soon come to realize that when it comes to deciding on which KPIs to use, each project may require different yardsticks as no two projects are the same.

There are three most common types of metrics, which we discuss below:

1. Deliverables

Deliverables focus on the output of the whole Scrum team and the increment of value being provided to clients after each sprint. This measurement can take a number of forms but could include time saved, a reduction in costs or driving sales. It can be any deliverable that directly adds value to the client. Such deliverables can also be measured in terms of the specific functionality they provide. Let's run through, more specifically, how you could use deliverable metrics to measure your team's success:

a. Sprint Success: The success in achieving a sprint goal is a metric from the agile framework, which enables a team to determine if the specific sprint they have just completed, met the required standard, and increment of output. In order to draw a conclusion, teams should begin by highlighting what the main objective of the sprint was. If user stories are well drafted and clear, this objective should be easy for the team to pin point and agree on.

The team should also spend time deciding on what actions and resources are needed to achieve the sprint goal, as well as agreeing on how they will know if the goal has been achieved. If they come to the conclusion that the goal has in fact been met, the sprint retrospective should make a note of how this was done for future reference. Ultimately, this is considered accomplished if the sprint's outcome aligns with the user story/criteria outlined in the product backlog.

b. *Escaped Defects*: This is a metric that focuses on the number of bugs or defects, which the developers encountered during the development of a particular product. Using this metric is common when a product is reliant on testing to ensure that it has the required functionality.

c. *The density of Defects*: Related to the previous metrics, defect density focuses on the number of bugs that presented themselves per given unit of production. If a team is implementing Scrum in the process of manufacturing, defect density could relate to the number of errors that occurred for a given amount of quantity to be produced. This metric is useful when comparing individual sprints as well as comparing individual final products.

d. *Velocity*: Velocity is a metric, which is rather particular to Scrum. Velocity refers to the number of user stories or criteria, which are completed during a sprint. It is important to note that this is not an absolute metric in the sense that it can allow for comparison. For example, the completion of two stories within one sprint may be far more impressive (depending on the complexity of the criteria) than the completion of three stories (if the criteria were relatively simple to solve). Nevertheless, this is a useful measurement in tracking the speed at which the development team is able to work.

e. *Sprint Burndown*: As we know, a sprint burndown is the measure of the total hours required by a sprint divided by the number of workdays available. The burndown chart shows hours available for the sprint depleting at the days of the sprint tick by. It is a graphical representation of the team's progress. If the development team runs smoothly and no obstacles present themselves, teams may find that there is no need to work overtime. If a team does encounter issues, and overtime hours are needed, this is also included in the burndown chart.

Effectiveness KPIs measure the overall effectiveness of the Scrum team and their related success. There is a long list of metrics that fall under metrics including Return on Investment (or ROI) or the time it took to get a product to market. Effective KPIs measure success by evaluating how a team's actions had a direct positive impact on the business they are developing for, or possibly even the impact created on an entire industry.

1. *Time to Market:* The time it takes for a product to reach the stage of becoming an income generating product for a client is referred to as the time to market. In Scrum terms, this is the number of sprints it takes a development team to get a product to its release date and to a point where it starts to generate income. Time to market is a metric that becomes more significant as a project's increases in scope and time to release date.

2. *ROI*: This metric measures the cost of a project versus the price paid by the client for development. A Scrum team, for example, may be employed by a company to develop products for its clients. The ROI for the company employing the team would be measured by comparing the cost of each sprint versus the price paid for the final product by the client. The costs for each sprint would include items such as wages, hardware, software, and any other cost associated with producing the final product.

From a client's perspective, the client will compare the price paid for the development of the product and compare it to income, which the final product generates. The cost of Scrums is usually calculated by breaking them down into sprints. This makes it easier for the product owner and Scrum manager to keep track of the overall cost of a project and the expenses incurred by the development team. The tracking of expenses during Scrum implementation is usually done through the use of a comprehensive spreadsheet.

3. *Redeployment of Capital:* Deployment of capital refers to the purchase of new capital at the beginning of a project, which is needed for product development. Redeployment of capital refers to an instance where there is a need for additional capital, which arises midway through a project. This can be tricky to navigate as having to make an unexpected purchase of software can affect the viability of the project for the Scrum team. If, however, the requirement is due to the increased scope of the project due to a change in client demands, this will be taken into consideration.

4. *Client Satisfaction:* Having a client who is satisfied and happy with the final product of a sprint is a team's main objective. This does not refer to the individuals who would use the product, but rather to the individual who paid for the product developed. Achieving a positive end resulted is aided by the requirements of Scrum teams to develop with an iterative approach and regular feedback. To get a broader picture of the team's success, client satisfaction could be combined with metrics such as ROI.

The Scrum Team

Evaluating the Scrum team itself and its individual members can provide insights into how successful they are a team. This requires looking at things such as individual job satisfaction, attrition and turnover, and the skills developed within the team. Using this information, the product owner and Scrum master can make educated decisions on the most effective way to manage the team's progress and whether the development could be sped up or slowed down.

When it comes to Scrum, although the processes and equipment used in the development of a product are important, it is the human element of the team that is the most crucial ingredient. Ensuring the happiness and health of the Scrum team should be done on a regular basis. Each role within Scrum is equally as important as the next. While some may consider the development team to be the most important part of the Scrum team, achieving success would be unlikely without a talented Scrum master and product owner.

The above three categories, though they are broad in definition, are useful to understand and use as a means to evaluate how a team is performing and whether or not the implementation and operation of the Scrum framework are proving beneficial and effective.

Chapter Six

User Stories

The concept of a user story or a user requirement developed as a result of the collaboration of developers and business specialists. Typically, when a problem arose leading to a development project, and the objectives needed to be defined, software developers would over-analyze the requirements, while software developers would typically not conduct an analysis that was thorough enough. Although both teams are highly skilled in their individual areas, this often created delays in starting a project. Prior to user stories, they existed in the form of user requirements.

User Requirements – the traditional definition

User requirements were defined as a list of required criteria for a system to abide by. Most traditional criteria related to business processes and were imposed on the system, which typically related to its conditions, constraints, and capabilities. These user requirements had to abide by certain standards:

1. Presentation: user requirements were defined in text and very seldom by graphical representation

2. Business Perspective: requirements were drafted from the perspective of the business and its needs

3. Comprehensive: requirements were to be written in such a way to ensure they did not include open ended requirements

4. Capable of being tested: the requirements had to be of the nature to make provision for testing

5. Specific: they were drafted with as much detail as possible to ensure no room for doubt and ambiguity

User requirements were traditionally drafted with the purpose of defining exactly how a system should operate. They were written using the narrative of "Shall." An example would be: 'A system shall include numbers between 1 and 1000 only.' These requirements were rigid in nature and not intended to be changed or edited. During their compilation, the objective was to specify their detail, and with finality before coding or development would commence.

From User Requirements to Use Cases

A new version of user requirements developed as software development methodologies matured. Use cases took note of the interactions of a user (or actor) with a particular system and the corresponding action, which the system delivered. User cases, unlike user requirements, now included more than just text descriptions and had two main components:

- Descriptions: the descriptions of use cases were much less restrictive and rigid than user requirements. Instead of the narrative using "shall," stories were written in such a way that they would describe a user's actions followed by how they would expect the system to react.

As the overall realm of system design and software development became more mature and complex, there was a change in thinking that ultimately altered how user requirements, or later user cases, were constructed. The new thinking which guided the process was that the end result of the project or system design should aim to make the life of the client or user easier (and not necessarily the developer).

This led to a change to user-centric systems. While the main elements of user requirements remained, they were developed further to include still a detailed interaction between a user and a system but to focus on what value the system brings to the user. User requirement drafters found that the best way to achieve this focus on value was to use metaphors to define requirements. This is how the process evolved to what we now know as user stories.

User Stories are born

User stories set out to define each requirement metaphorically by compiling them using the following form: 'As a (user role), I want a (desired feature of functionality) so that (value or benefit).'

The user role highlights in what capacity the user will be making use of the desired functionality. The desired feature describes exactly what that user in their specific role wishes to achieve and the value or benefit highlights exactly what the resulting outcome will be.

User stories, through the use of metaphors, focus on the work the system should be doing for the user and do not include detailed features that are required to be built into the system. In other words, the biggest change in user stories compared to user requirements or cases is a change in focus on the value, which a particular story would bring to a user without prescribing HOW this value should be delivered. User stories are less detailed and precise in their definition for this reason.

During a Scrum project, user stories will undergo a number of changes and transformations relating to how much detail they contain. Within the agile context, user stories are the result of collaborative conversations amongst developers and product owners.

Regardless of the project management methodology, you choose to use for a project; user stories can be extremely useful. For agile projects, they are the tool of choice when it comes to gathering requirements for a number of reasons, including:

- User stories gather requirements with the main focus on the user of the final product. This focus ensures a higher level of client satisfaction as delivering functionality to make their lives easier is constantly at the forefront of the developer's minds.

- They simplify requirements to bridge the gap between business professionals and software developers. The narrative of phrasing requirements using the simple approach of "I want-," "So that I can-," forces developers to consider the viewpoint of the client and phrase the project using solutions that are practical and useable in the real world.

- User stories are concise in the way they are written, which aid in creating a focus for the development team and prevent paralysis by analysis but excluding too much detail.

- User stories can be easily understood by all members of the team. This is an improvement from user cases whose graphical representations and explanations were not always easy to digest.

- Through using an iterative approach, where stories are edited and changed throughout the development process, user stories are enhanced and improved upon, as opposed to being codified in the early stages of development (as with user requirements).

- As user stories involve the whole team and require a collaborative approach, making use of stories ensures a certain level of teamwork and a shared understanding of what needs to be accomplished.

It is clear the many numbers of advantages which user stories can provide development teams. Yet, there are still a number of project management teams who do not favor making use of user stories. These reasons include:

- Some development teams are accustomed to using client requirements, which contain more detail and find user stories too brief.

- When requirements for a project are complex, a written criteria requirement may not be sufficient. Some teams may require supporting documentation or notes for their team to understand what they are trying to achieve fully.

These limitations should be taken into consideration by project management professionals when deciding whether or not to make use of user stories for their upcoming projects. Now that we understand their evolution let's look into the rules, which should be followed when making use of user stories.

User Story Best Practice

In 2003 Bill Wake, one of the pioneers of the Agile methodology created an acronym to guide teams in creating effective stories. This acronym was **INVEST** and is broken down as follows:

- **Independent:** user stories should be compiled in a way that makes them independent from each other, and overlapping should be avoided where possible. If user stories are interlinked, it may prove difficult for teams to schedule their completion, as the completion of one story may relay on the successful completion of a separate story.

- **Negotiable:** User Stories are ever changing and, as such, are negotiable. They are allowed to change as the requirements of the project change. They are also created through robust conversations between all internal stakeholders, which provide a shared team vision.

- **Valuable:** A rule of thumb for user stories is that, unless they provide clear and tangible value to the project, they should not be included. Similarly, user stories that do provide value but are not well articulated should be fleshed out and rephrased in a way that makes them aid the project.

- **Estimation:** User stories, in order to be successful, must be drafted in such a way that allows for the team to estimate the length of time and effort that will be needed to complete them with relative ease.

- **Scalable:** Scrum teams aim to keep their length between 2 and 4 weeks long. This requires that user stories, in the way they are drafted, should be of such a nature that they can be successfully completed during the sprint. A user story that cannot be completed within a sprint is generally considered to be of poor quality.

- **Testable:** the final rule or guideline for drafting user stories is that the criteria or task which the story contains should be able, once completed, to be tested. Without this capability, it is of little value to the development team.

These guidelines above will assist you in ensuring there is structure within the stories your team produces and set your team up to develop high-quality output. When beginning the compiling of stories as a team, it may be challenging, at least initially, to determine which user stories are not up to standard. By going back to the above guidelines and ensuring each user story abides by them, your team can ensure they are on the right track to start a successful sprint.

Chapter Seven

Mastering Scrum

Now that you are equipped with the foundational knowledge of Scrum and have perhaps started its implementation through your project management role, we want to build on this knowledge and provide our best tips and advice for, not only implementing Scrum, but mastering it.

1. Encourage Collaboration

Although all team members should conduct themselves in a manner that lends itself to team collaboration, this is ultimately the responsibility of the Scrum master. A Scrum master cannot be effective in their role without clearly promoting and facilitating collaboration between team members. They should provide guidance and work together with the product owner on any issues, which arise, which may affect the progress of the development. Although encouraging collaboration and working closely with others may not come naturally to members new to Scrum, this is a skill that should be nurtured and developed.

For a Scrum master to successfully tackle their role, especially if new to the position, a good starting point would be to focus on the best ways to assist the product owner in working on and reviewing the product backlog and then encourage team collaboration based on the content of the product backlog.

2. Avoid Over Commitment

A team's enthusiasm and drive to complete the development of a project may lead them towards over committing during sprint planning and biting off more than they can chew. A tired and fatigued team may also want to get across the finish line for a project and over commit to what is reasonably achievable. Looking at previous sprint velocity is a good measure of how much the team can achieve.

In some cases, the product owner may not be the first to restrict the team in the commitment to achieve an unrealistic amount of work during a sprint. This could be due to their commitments to the client or business and will to impress and deliver timeously. In this instance, it is the responsibility of the Scrum master to dissuade teams from over committing. Overcommitting can have a lasting negative impact on a team's development and motivation, as not being able to achieve what is set out during a sprint could leave team members feeling deflated and under accomplished.

Having open channels of communications between the Scrum master, product owner, and development team are crucial in ensuring that teams do not over commit. Should the Scrum master have such concerns, they should be able to articulate and explain their viewpoint in such a way as to facilitate understanding and that they could be over-committing without being overbearing.

3. Be aware of task details

Scrum promotes collaboration and teamwork. This can become tricky if team members are not fully aware of what their team members are working on. As a project manager using Scrum, part of your responsibility includes understanding what each team member is working on and ensuring that their team members are also informed. Both the product owner and/or project manager should place themselves in a position where rendering assistance to the team is done easily. Offering regular support and showing genuine interest in what each person is working on will set the tone for a great working ethos.

4. Main Focus and Stay Balanced Throughout

Maintaining a team's focus is key when tackling complex tasks within a development project. The short nature of sprints makes maintaining the focus of a team significantly easier. It is highly unlikely that a completed product can be completed in one sprint. It is the onus of the Scrum master to ensure that all attention is on delivering the increment of product at hand, and that team members do not become concerned by other elements of delivery outside the parameters of the current sprint. Although teams will be aware of future items on the product backlog, these should not be in focus when working on a specific unrelated item.

The Scrum master should consistently remind the team of the task at hand and also create a focus on the current goal. The goal and all of its elements should always be made clear to all team members. This will serve as a reminder should team members feel distracted. It may be useful to set up physical reminders on a notice board that is clearly visible and can be reviewed during and after daily Scrums.

When it comes to ensuring that the development of a quality product is maintained and is balanced, this is the joint responsibility of the product owner and Scrum master to achieve this. The Scrum master should ensure that the quality of the product is not compromised through the efforts of improving the team. The Scrum master should ensure that the pursuance of quality is maintained. While the product owner's biggest objective is to ensure the most viable and high-quality product is produced, they need to work with the Scrum master to ensure that the best development Scrum practices are deployed.

It may be tempting for a product owner to instruct a team to overlook or skip certain best practices during development for the sake of time and meeting deadlines, but this is to be avoided. All roles within the process should ensure they work towards maintaining a balance between delivering a product of the highest possible quality while also making use of Scrum best practices.

5. Be Bold in Pushing Boundaries

Regardless of the current morale of a team, whether they feel they are going through a dip in motivation and progress, or are flying high in terms of achieving their goal, all teams benefit and require motivation and a push to achieve at increasingly higher levels. Teams should be reminded of their potential to achieve better results by opening themselves up to all possibilities.

Managing the morale of a Scrum team is a balancing act between offering support when team members are stretched to their limits, and providing additional positive pressure when you are aware they are not pushing themselves enough. By taking the time to really understand how teams operate and what forms of motivation they respond to, you will be able to get the most out of a team whether you are a Scrum master or project manager.

It is important to note that motivation is not the sole responsibility of these main roles within agile but also falls on all individual members of a team. They should encourage and support one another to achieve the highest possible level of output. This often has a snowball effect as team members will thrive by not only receiving support from key roles but also lateral support from those working alongside them. Team members should also hold one another accountable for commitments made and for attaining desired standards of output.

6. Build a Team with Varying Skills

Some of the most successful teams and resultant products were created by encouraging teams to transfer skills and knowledge amongst all members. Those working on a defined project should have varied skill sets to ensure that the product built is of a high standard. In terms of the Scrum methodology, this is a key principle. Each project will have certain elements or obstacles to overcome, which are best tackled by team members, which more specialized or advanced skills.

It is for this reason that a software team of generalists or jack-of-all-trades does not always create products of the highest quality. All teams need to team players possess more knowledge or expertise on certain elements of the development process. These skills could include quality assurance testing, business analysis skills, design, or data management. The Scrum master should ensure that, during the recruitment process or compiling of Scrum teams, that all the necessary skills are covered collectively by the team.

7. Create an environment conducive to success

As a Scrum master, there is a lot you can do to ensure that the working environment for a Scrum project is conducive to members not only feeling motivated, but also having fun. Such an environment will spark creativity and allow the team to better deal with any stress related to the project and unwind when necessary. Being approachable and personable as the Scrum master falls part of creating the desired work environment. Team members who genuinely feel like they can communicate or approach the Scrum master with any problems they have will be more successful in executing their tasks.

8. Promote Autonomy

From the start of the development process, right until the end, the development team should be coached by both the product owner and/or project manager to allow them to develop self-organizing and self-leading skills. Even new team members, who may start a project as newcomers to Scrum, should develop the skills and know-how of self-organization.

The main reason why the Scrum framework does not provide for one direct manager is to ensure the self-reliance and growth of a team's autonomy. The joint efforts of the scum master and project manager should encourage this. Should these key roles be absent for a period of time during the development process, teams should be able to continue independently with a comprehensive and mutual understanding of the tasks they ought to be focusing on. As teams become accustomed to this way of working as a team, they will improve through each sprint and gain confidence in their autonomy. The thread of self-organization should run through every aspect of the team's operation and should be supported continuously supported by the product owner and Scrum master (and project manager where applicable).

While it may be tempting to jump in and assist teams by completing tasks for them, this undermines the Scrum framework and will create dependence, an unwanted element of this project management framework.

9. Nurture relationships with Team Members

As with taking ownership of creating a productive and happy environment, a Scrum master or project manager should do what they can to encourage comradery and friendship amongst team members. Although there is a limit on creating synergy between team members who do not particularly like each other, opening up dialogue and communication between team members is important. Allow and encourage members to find common ground on personal interests and encourage socialization when the team is not hard at work. When teams have members who have developed relationships and friendships, they are able to produce at a level that exceeds limitations and sets higher standards.

10. Know the Blind Spots

A great advantage of managing teams is having a good understanding of both the strengths and weaknesses of all individual team members, as well as the blind spots of the team as a whole. This will allow a Scrum master to better guide the team in determining what can reasonably be achieved during a sprint as well as assist in making decisions throughout the development process.

Knowing exactly what a team is capable of will make it easier to determine if a team and its individual members are overly ambitious or not ambitious enough. The extent to which a team can be pushed during a sprint can also be decided upon with a good understanding of strengths and weaknesses.

11. Educate the Team on Scrum Tools

There are many Scrum tools available to a Scrum master or project manager to manage a Scrum team or development process best. These tools include burn up charts, burn down charts, velocity tracking, and story mapping. It is important to ensure that a team not only understands their roles but also knows how to use the tools at their disposal. These tools store information, which can make the process of development more streamlined and easier to execute upon. Scrum tools improve workflow and productively. Wherever possible and affordable, teams should be taught and encouraged to use as many Scrum management tools as they have access to, and which can enhance their development process.

How to deal with Resistance to Scrum

Many team members resist the change to Scrum for a number of different reasons. For some, it may be because they are accustomed to the way they currently work and the colleagues they work with. It may feel like it has taken them time to work their way up to a particular role or level within an organization, and they may feel like making a big change in the way a team works or organizes themselves may jeopardize this. They may feel like they have a good grip on the work they currently do and don't want to lose cadence by changing frameworks.

Other reasons for resisting the change to Scrum may be because of fear of the unknown or possibly that they simply dislike or distrust the practices and principles of Scrum. Regardless of the reason, each act of resistance offers a reason as to how people really feel about Scrum. Should you be responsible for implementing the change to Scrum, it is your responsibility as a leader to ensure that you understand exactly why there is resistance. This is an opportunity for you to learn from it and assist that team member in overcoming their reservations or concerns.

When it comes to implementing change within an organization, resistance is an inevitable part of the process. What is crucial is how the leaders within the organization deal with the resistance. Instead of viewing resistance as an obstacle to be overcome, leaders should rather take it as an opportunity to take input onboard, which could serve as warnings or weaknesses. When resistance is present, it is the time for leaders to listen and explore what those team members are voicing as their reasons.

In handling resistance, leaders within an organization should be wary of creating an atmosphere that is 'us' versus 'them.' The best approach is to find common ground and create a platform or environment where concerns can be raised freely and honestly. Take note of what each team a member is raising as a reason for resistance and give them assurance it has been taken onboard. This approach will make navigating the change of a project management framework that much easier.

Chapter Eight

Scrum Management Errors to Avoid

Although the Scrum principles are simple and relatively easy to grasp, there are a number of common errors that occur. These are relatively easy to avoid once they have been identified.

1. Underestimating the effort involved in switching to Scrum/Agile
After getting an initial understanding of Scrum and its key principles and tools, a project manager may be of the impression that making the transition to Scrum may be a seamless process. Although Scrum is a simple framework to grasp, a successful transition involves more conscious effort and determination that anticipated. In more complex situations, the problems to be overcome may require greater levels of Scrum management expertise and commitment to follow through until the initial speed bumps are overcome.

The fast pace of Scrum with an expected high level of outputs can take a team some time to adjust to. There may also be higher levels of stress associated with the move to agile, which a project manager may not anticipate. The recommended approach is to expect the transition to be messy and allow for extended lead times due to delays and frustrations with the change. Changes to the way a team collaborates can often undercover underlying organizational issues that need resolving. These commonly include poor communication, lack of trust, and lack of accountability.

Encountering these issues and overcoming them may seem daunting at first, but by approaching them head-on, a team will be more successful in the long run. The key to overcoming these challenges is to expect that they may arise and initially delay the effects and implementation of Scrum. Do not be deterred as the nature of Scrum and its focus on teamwork, transparency, and accountability will continue to address and eradicate common problems within teams that may have already been present.

2. Implementation without adhering to the Rules
Many teams will implement Scrum under the direction of a project manager, and initially be educated and well-versed in all the key elements and practices of Scrum, including making use of Scrum artifacts, having daily Scrums, and ensuring consistent communication between team members. As projects progress and teams become fatigued, it is tempting for teams to slowly loosen the practices and use of the tools, which they initially abided by. Many organizations fall short of the requirement to consistently implement all the elements of Scrum.

Not only is it important that the practices that are integral to Scrum are followed, but it is important that the principles explained at the beginning of this guide, which underpins these practices, are consistently discussed and understood.

3. Creating Unnecessary Complications
As you implement Scrum and get used to using as an over-arching framework, it may be tempting to allow other practices and smaller

frameworks to creep into your everyday operations. While facilitating the parallel use of other frameworks with Scrum is one of its many positive attributes, it is important to keep the implementation of Scrum as simple as possible.

Collaboration and enhancement tools are constantly being released to make Scrum easier to implement. Although it may be tempting to delve straight into buying or to use these tools, make sure you do not spend precious time implementing tools when refining the simple elements of Scrum would be a better use of your time and energy.

4. Using the Scrum Master as a Messenger

As the Scrum master communicates with the team as a whole, and individually on a one on one basis, it may occur that team members start to use the Scrum master as a messenger, as opposed to exercising their duty to communicate openly and honestly with other teammates. Developers could also, through their naturally more regular interaction with the Scrum master, direct any questions they have relating to, for example, a user story, to the Scrum master as opposed to directly to the product owner.

This kind of communication should be prevented at all costs as it undermines one of the key principles of Scrum relating to always having open channels of communication. This indirect communication can also relate to timewasting as, in this example, the Scrum master would have to contact the product owner first and then relay the answer to the developer. A must more efficient option would be for the developer to contact the product owner directly. If indirect communication is left to continue, it could cause miscommunication between the team as a whole.

Chapter Nine

Methodology Comparisons and Scrum Management Tools

Scrum Vs. Other Methodologies:

The debate as to which project methodologies are most effective is a common one in recent times. Developers will often enter long discussions on the difference between traditional software development methods and Agile software development to determine which is superior. As you are embarking on the Scrum journey, it is good to understand exactly how it differs from the traditional approach.

What are the traditional project management methodologies?

A good starting point is a definition of the traditional software development model and what it entails. Waterfall methodology, where we have already introduced, is often what people are referring to when they mention traditional software development. Originating in the 1950s, the waterfall is widely used by many development teams across different projects. This methodology is based on three main principles, namely low levels of client engagement, thorough project documentation, and structuring projects in a sequential manner.

When it comes to involving their clients, waterfall teams usually only hold two meetings with their clients during a project. The first meeting is before the project starts and the second is conducted only after the final software product is complete and is ready to be released. The second principle of the waterfall, relating to the strong project documentation, is necessary from the initiation of a project because of the low levels of client engagement. All requirements and their smaller details need to be carefully documented during the first meeting to ensure the team stays on track.

The third principle, relating to sequential phases, means that each project is broken down into 5 to 7 phases, which are performed one after another. The downside is that a development team cannot return to a previous stage of project realization even if they found that something went wrong.

How does Scrum differ?

As we know, Scrum is based on the key principles of good communication, regular client feedback loops, and a focus on an iterative approach to development. Compared to traditional methodologies that have bigger teams and more specialized individual members, Scrum has smaller teams comprised of members who may be specialized, but have also been able to operate across functions. A client has its own representative in the Scrum team in the form of the product owner who is responsible for compiling the backlog. Through an iterative process, the client is able to review the product increment after each sprint, which is a significant change from the two client meetings, which take place in traditional methodologies.

Now that we have covered the key differences between Scrum and traditional project management methodologies let's look into what other options exist under the Agile Framework.

Kanban

Kanban is a framework that was developed by a Toyota engineer by the name of Taaichi Ohno. In the 1940s, Toyota began to pay close attention to the way in which supermarkets restocked their shelves based on the level of consumer consumption. This effective way of responding to the market lead Toyota to develop a supply system in which production is driven by factual consumer consumption. This concept, of refraining from producing a surplus, is a key principle of the Kanban methodology. Kanban makes use of cards and a Kanban board to visualize how resources progress through the production cycle. The objective is to provide maximum visibility and insight into the development process to assist the manager in correcting product surpluses and deficits in real-time.

Kanban ascribes to the concept of "pull" rather than "push," which results in workers "pulling in" work according to their capacity. This is opposed to the workload being determined by what is delivered to them on the conveyor belt and subsequently becomes worker's to-do list. In software development, this "pull" notion means that a limit is placed on the volume of work that can be handled at one time. Kanban Cards, which contain elements of a project to be worked on, may be limited within the "In progress" stage of production. This is decrease multitasking and increases focus on the work at hand. Kanban, in a similar way to Scrum, is driven by the client's needs and revolves around constant communication. The product is only produced if it is certain to add value to the client. Kanban, besides being guided by higher levels of focus and placing the needs of the client first, places importance on decreasing waste throughout the development process.

One of the key differences between Kanban and Scrum is the continuous approach that Kanban takes compared to the iterative approach by Scrum. Kanban is often a better project management methodology to implement for teams who have unplanned work on the horizon, such as support issues or urgent and unplanned client requests. Kanban will allow these teams to begin work on projects as they appear, as opposed to needing a fuller picture of all the work to be completed.

Lean Software Development
Similar to Kanban, Lean focuses on reducing waste and focusing on the customer. Waste during a software development project could include multitasking, spending time building the wrong feature, or building a feature that will not be used. Two shared features between Lean and Kanban are the elements that are "pull" as well as maintaining respect for all team members throughout the development process. Lean is less strict or prescriptive in terms of delivery time boxes as the team is ready to deliver on a product or increment at any time.

Lean differs from Agile with its concept of Minimal Viable Product (MVP). This is the first version that is released as soon as possible and focuses on the notion of failing fast and making a development decision that is binding as late in the process as possible.

XP – Extreme Programming
XP is the most specific of all of the Agile methodologies. It aims to produce the highest quality product possible while ensuring it is not at

the expense of the developer's well-being. There are five main values that XP prescribes to mainly communication, simplicity, feedback, courage, and respect. XP focuses on using a number of different practices that are reliant on each other. This has meant that XP has received a lot of criticism as a methodology. All XP practices must be used together, or else it is not as successful as a framework.

In contract to methodologies such as waterfall, XP has the client present for most of the development process, which can prove stressful for many teams. There is also less emphasis on project requirements through the use of, for example, the product backlog, which is used in Scrum. Some consider this to be ineffective. Similar to Kanban and Lean, XP also focuses on a zero-waste approach by only writing code on the day it is needed, as opposed to forecasting what might be needed in the future and opening up the possibility it would be wasted.

Agile teams may use a number of different features and practices from Scrum, Lean, Kanban, Lean, and XP, and it may be difficult to pinpoint which particular one they ascribe to. This brief introduction to the other agile frameworks has hopefully provided you with some more context of the Scrum methodology.

Three of the Best Agile Team Management Tools

With the flexibility but maintained organization, which the Scrum methodology requires, it may take a Scrum team some time to get into a decent development cadence. For this reason, there are many software tools and programs that can significantly aid in streamlining and facilitating a team's progress. Although the market is flooded with many options, here are our five most agile (pun intended) software tools to implement agile methodologies.

1. Jira

Jira, a software developed by Atlassian, allows teams to plan, track, and manage agile projects and has been designed specifically for the agile methodology. Scrum teams are able to create user stories, and issues then set up the appropriate tasks. Process flows are easy to track, and stories are easy to prioritize. Although Jira is geared towards software development, it can be used in other departments across organizations. Jira supports Scrum, kanban as well as other hybrid combinations.

Pros:

- Once team members are familiar with Jira and its setup, this tool is invaluable in assisting and facilitating team cohesion and velocity.

- At a glance, team members are able to see exactly what other team members are working on due to the user-friendly interface of Jira. Tasks or projects that move through development stages can be dragged and dropped into the next stage.

- Jira also provides extensive training and community support to users to assist in mastering some of the complexity of the software

Cons:

- It can take users new to Jira some time to grasp the various elements involved in collaborating on the platform. This time can often not be spared by smaller businesses but may be accommodated by larger businesses that can facilitate training.

- The setup of the platform itself is time intensive

- A recent software upgrade from Jira has proved to be problematic.

2. Smartsheet

Smartsheet is a collaboration and project management software that allows teams to plan, track, and manage the projects they are working on in real-time. It provides teams with the capabilities to manage resources, create reports, and track progress using timelines.

Pros:

- Smartsheet continues to provide additional integrations with our software and tools with its platform

- Users can easily switch between different views of the same data set using grids, graphs, and tables.

- The platform offers extensive training and certifications

Cons:

- Multi-user editing can be difficult, and no formatting can take place in input cells when adding information

- There is no desktop app integration

- No feature within the doc, which is similar to a document. This means some users will overcrowd cells to include all relevant details. This can make reporting more complicated.

3. Asana

Asana is a cloud-based project management software tool that enables organizations to manage and organize tasks through active collaboration. It is a suitable option for businesses of any size and is able to handle multiple projects at one time. The main features of Asana include task management, dashboards, document management, and task assigning. It can be used on the desktop as well as mobile.

Pros:

- Users have many ways of accessing their to-do lists du to Asana's accessibility on multiple devices.

- It is relatively inexpensive compared to other platforms

- A large degree of customization is allowed which means it can suit the unique needs of many different businesses.

Cons:

- The notification systems around messages or overdue projects are not as prominent as it could be. Messages and notifications easily go unnoticed unless a user is constantly logged into Asana.

- As with many other agile project management tools, it takes users some time to be accustomed to using the platform and making use of its full functionality.

- Every task assigned in Asana generates an email notification that many users have found to be inefficient in keeping them on track due to the volume of emails this creates in their mailbox.

Although the above project management tools are useful for the mastery of Scrum, they are not crucial to its success. Getting accustomed to using new software and educating individual team members may take more time, and therefore money, than what justifies what they can provide you and your team. Ensure that you do a full analysis before making the financial investment in software.

Chapter Ten

Scaling of Scrum

The term scalability refers to the process of taking a defined process or framework and expanding upon the process so as to create a larger impact. Some processes or practices are easier to scale than others, and often the question is raised as to whether or not Scrum is scalable, and if so, how is this best done. Scaling Scrum, for example, could involve taking mechanisms from one Scrum team and implementing them in multiple teams for larger projects.

So, the question is, 'Is Scrum scalable?' Initially, Scrum was thought only to be applicable to teams who work on smaller projects, and that is was not suitable for application across multiple teams for larger projects. However, this was only based on the fact that Scrum had not yet been used on larger scale projects, and since its inception Scrum has been applied and successfully scaled.

So, when and how should a team make a move to scale a Scrum project? The answer to this question usually depends on the nature of the project and at what level a team would like to scale. Scaling usually occurs at one of three different levels as scaling can take place across projects, programs, or portfolios. Depending on what level a team would like to scale at determines how much coordination is required.

When it comes to scalability, additional resources and project managers may be necessary to ensure that development stays on track.

When it comes to Scrum teams, it is usually recommended that teams stay under ten members. In the event that an organization wishes to scale their Scrum projects, it is recommended that a bigger team is divided into smaller groups who meet regularly to discuss their progress and report any issues or concerns. Keeping cadence with these meetings and ensuring they happen at regular intervals is crucial and could be managed by a project manager.

We previously discussed the Scrum of Scrums, which is where multiple teams synchronize their projects. Each Scrum team would select a team representative who join the Scrum meetings and update on the team's progress, challenges they may be facing, breakthroughs they may have had, as well as coordinate any future activities with other teams. When it comes to deciding how often a Scrum of Scrums should meet, it is the size of the project, level of interdependency, complexity, and recommendations from upper management, which should be taken into consideration.

As we know, Scrum recommends that meetings and collaboration take place face to face. Although not impossible to implement Scrum over different geographical locations, it does take a lot more coordination and effort. When it comes to scaling a project with teams in different offices, the Scrum of Scrum meeting scan takes place using video conferencing tools. When larger projects are deployed, a chief of Scrums will need to hire, and this person is responsible for facilitating all the sessions between the Scrum of Scrums. The chief of Scrums will determine exactly when meetings should take place and outline their agendas. These meetings, like other check-ins, will involve the sharing of updates on progress, challenges, and recognized dependencies across projects. Once teams receive an agenda from the chief Scrum master, they should prepare their updates ahead of the meeting. Should any particular members of a team be facing challenges, these should be raised in these meetings, as it is often likely that other teams may experience the same challenges. This allows teams to share in problem solving and overcome obstacles at a quicker rate.

When these meetings take place, each team representative will usually provide an update that answers four main questions. These include what the team has been working on since the last meetings, what the team plans to work on between now and the next meeting, asking other representatives if there are any other elements of development the other teams dependent on them for, and finally, what could the team be working on that would directly impact the other teams.

The outcome of these Scrum of Scrum meetings is usually better coordination of work, which is carried out across teams. This is specifically true when there are tasks that run across different teams, and there are high levels of dependency. This ensures that if there are any obstacles, discrepancies between expectations, or change in deliverables, they are exposed and addressed as soon as possible. These meetings also operate as an open forum when representatives can provide honest feedback and receive recommendations or input from other representatives.

In the event that a project is scaled above the capabilities of a Scrum of Scrums framework, an additional meeting framework is created where a representative from each Scrum of Scrums is sent to a larger meeting known as the 'Scrum of Scrum of Scrums.' This allows all projects that are related to each other to be coordinated in such a way that allows for maximum quality and timeous output. What is important to note is that this type of coordination, especially should the larger teams be distributed across geographical locations, will require much larger coordination and management effort.

Conclusion

I hope this book was able to help you to gain an understanding of Scrum principles, practices, and underlying values. By taking the opportunity to learn more about Scrum, you are starting the journey of bigger opportunities as you execute on project delivery of the highest standard, relying on the values which underpin Scrum. You should have the knowledge to not only teach members of your team about Scrum and its events and processes, but also have the foundation to continue to build upon for your Scrum and project management career.

If you are an individual looking to become skilled in the realm of project management, then you have taken a big step towards being a seasoned professional on the execution of agile, and more specifically, Scrum. The next step is to continue to learn about Scrum through the process of implementation and continuous learning and education. Pursuing a formal certification is one way to take the next step in your project management career. Alternatively, you could simply use what you have learned through reading this guide to implement the valuable processes and practices of Scrum in any of the projects you may work on going forward.

The agile framework is an advocate for continuous learning and improvement of teams and what they can produce. Whether you strictly follow the rules and guidelines you have read here to implement Scrum, or simply extract only those that are applicable to you specifically, you will be taking a positive step towards you and your team's growth and improvement. What is important is that, in line with agile learning precept, you should pass as much knowledge to your team members throughout the Scrum process.

Once you have created your Scrum team and initiated the development process, you can fine-tune and tweak the process to correct for any inconsistencies or challenges you or your team may face. Keep in mind that you may have a number of different challenges, which you may face in the initial stages of Scrum implementation. This is par for the course and over time will lead your team to be more established and effective in product development. Remember to be patient, get help from an agile coach if needed, and enjoy the process and newly acquired skills.

The next step, following the mastering of this guide, could be to enlist in a Scrum project management certification of which there are many. These are most commonly divided into the three main roles within the Scrum framework, depending on which role you choose to pursue, as well as qualifications. For example, implementing Scrum and integrating it with Kanban. Although the implementation of Scrum is relatively easy, the mastering of Scrum takes more patience and effort. Pursuing a qualification may provide you with further confidence to confidently lead a Scrum team, and complex development process as well as successfully scale the process for larger projects across multiple teams.

If you are a project manager in the traditional sense, you will still be able to use your broad set of skills to complement any Scrum team. Although debates still continue as to how your role may fit into Scrum, depending on your key skills, you will be a valuable asset to any Scrum team.

Made in the USA
Middletown, DE
15 March 2020